Mike M

C PROGRAMMING

Learn the ANSI C standard

In easy steps is an imprint of Computer Step
Southfield Road · Southam
Warwickshire CV47 0FB · United Kingdom
www.ineasysteps.com

Second Edition

Notice of Liability
Every effort has been made to ensure that this book contains accurate
and current information. However, Computer Step and the author
shall not be liable for any loss or damage suffered by readers as a
result of any information contained herein.

Trademarks
All trademarks are acknowledged as belonging to their respective
companies.

Printed and bound in the United Kingdom

ISBN-13 978-1-84078-323-0
ISBN-10 1-84078-323-0

Contents

1

Introducing C

Welcome to the world of C. This first chapter demonstrates how to create a C program in text form, then shows how to compile it into executable byte form.

The C language

C is a compact general-purpose programming language that was originally developed by Dennis Ritchie for the Unix operating system. It was first implemented on the Digital Equipment Corporation PDP-11 computer in 1972.

This new programming language was named "C" as it succeeded an earlier programming language named "B" that had been introduced around 1970.

The Unix operating system and virtually all Unix applications are written in the C language. However, C is not limited to a particular platform and programs can be created on any machine that supports C, including those employing the Windows platform.

The flexibility and portability of C made it very popular and the language was formalized in 1988 by the American National Standards Institute (ANSI). The ANSI C standard unambiguously defined each aspect of C, thereby eliminating some uncertainty about the precise syntax of the language.

ANSI C has become the recognized standard for the C language and is described, and demonstrated by examples, in this book.

Why learn C programming?

The C language has been around for quite some time and has seen the introduction of newer programming languages like Java, C++ and C#. Many of these new languages are derived, at least in part, from C, but are much larger in size. The more compact C is better to start out in programming because it is simpler to learn.

It is easier to move on to learn the newer languages once the principles of C programming have been grasped. For instance, C++ is an extension of C and can be difficult to learn unless you have mastered C programming first.

Despite the extra features available in newer languages C remains popular because it is versatile and efficient. It is used today on a large number of platforms for everything from micro-controllers to the most advanced scientific systems. Programmers around the world embrace C because it allows them maximum control and efficiency in their programs.

Standard C libraries

ANSI C defines a number of standard libraries that contain tried and tested functions which can be used in your own C programs.

The libraries are known as "header files" and each have the file extension of ".h". The names of the C standard library header files are listed in the table below with a description of their purpose.

Library	Description
stdio.h	Contains input and output functions, types and macro definitions. This library is used by most C programs and represents almost one third of the entire C library
ctype.h	Contains functions for testing characters
string.h	Contains functions for manipulating strings
math.h	Contains mathematical functions
stdlib.h	Contains utility functions for number conversion, storage allocation, etc.
assert.h	Contains a function that can be used to add diagnostics to a program
stdarg.h	Contains a function that can be used to step through a list of function arguments
setjmp.h	Contains a function that can be used to avoid the normal call and return sequence
signal.h	Contains functions for handling exceptional conditions that may arise in a program
time.h	Contains functions for manipulating date and time
limits.h	Contains constant definitions for the size of C data types
float.h	Contains constant definitions relating to floating-point arithmetic

Hot tip

A function is a piece of code that can be reused repeatedly in a C program. A description of each function in the C library is given in the Reference section, starting on page 161.

9

The GNU C compiler

C programs are initially created as plain text files, saved with the file extension of ".c". These can be written in any text editor, such as Windows Notepad – no special software is needed.

In order to execute a C program it must first be "compiled" into byte code that can be understood by the computer. A C compiler reads the original text version of the program and translates it into a second file – in a machine-readable executable format.

If the text program contains any syntax errors these will be reported by the compiler and the executable file will not be built.

One of the most popular C compilers is the GNU C compiler (GCC) that is available free under the terms of the General Public License (GPL). It is included with virtually every distribution of the Linux operating system. The GNU C compiler is used to compile all the example programs listed in this book into executable byte code.

To discover if you already have the GNU C compiler on your system type gcc -v at a command prompt. If available the compiler will respond with version information:

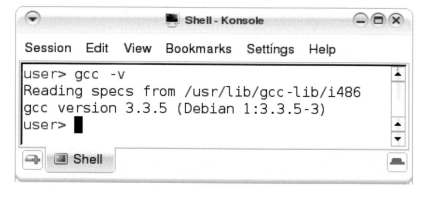

If you are using the Linux platform and the GNU C compiler is not available on your computer install it from the distribution CD-ROM, or ask your system administrator to install it for you.

If you are using the Windows platform you will need to install the GNU C compiler by following the instructions on the next page.

Hot tip

The complete terms and conditions of the General Public License can be found at http://www.gnu.org/copyleft/gpl.html.

Don't forget

f a C compiler is installed the standard C library header files (listed on the previous page) will also be installed.

Hot tip

Because C++ is an extension of C, any C++ development tool can also be used to compile C programs.

Installing GCC for Windows

The GNU (pronounced "guh-NEW") Project was launched in 1984 to develop a complete Unix-like operating system as free software. A part of the GNU system is the Minimalist GNU for Windows (MinGW) package. MinGW includes the GNU C compiler that can be used on Windows systems to create exccutable C programs. MinGW download information is at:

http://www.mingw.org/download.shtml

The MinGW distribution package is a single binary file named similarly to MinGW-3.1.0-1.exe – download the current version. After downloading the package, run the executable file and accept the suggested destination location to serve as the base of the installation (C:\MinGW).

Finally, add the C:\MinGW\bin sub-directory of the MinGW installation to your system PATH. In Windows XP open the Environment Variables dialog by clicking the System icon in the Control Panel then select the Advanced tab and push the Environment Variables button. Find the Path variable then edit the end of its statement line to include C:MinGW\bin.

Hot tip

GNU is a recursive acronym for "GNU's Not Unix".

Beware

On older versions of Windows add the C:\MinGW\bin address at the end of the Set Path statement in the C:\autoexec.bat file.

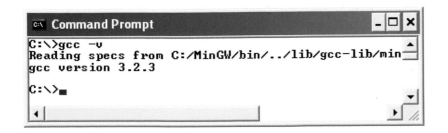

To verify that installation completed properly type gcc -v at a command prompt and the GNU C compiler will respond with version information:

A first C program

In C programs the code statements to be executed are contained inside "functions". Code that defines a function is called a function "declaration" and always has this syntax:

data-type function-name () { *statements-to-be-executed* }

After a function has been called upon to execute the statements it contains, it returns a value to the caller. This value can only be of the data-type specified in the function declaration.

A program can contain one or many functions but must always have a function called "main". The main() function is the starting point of all C programs and the C compiler will not compile the code unless it finds a function called "main" within the program.

Other functions in a program can be given any name you like using letters, digits and the underscore character, but the name may not begin with a digit. Also the C keywords, listed in the Handy Reference on the inner front cover of this book, must be avoided.

The plain brackets that follow the function-name can, optionally, contain values to be used by that function. These take the form of a comma-separated list and are known as function "arguments".

The curly brackets (braces) contain the statements to be executed whenever the function is called. Each statement must be terminated by a semi-colon, in the same way that English language sentences must be terminated by a full stop.

Traditionally, the first program to attempt when learning any programming language is that which simply generates the message "Hello World". In C, the program code looks like this:

```c
#include <stdio.h>

int main()
{
  printf("Hello World\n");
  return 0;
}
```

Notice how the code is formatted using spacing (known as whitespace) and indentation to improve its readability.

Beware

Avoid choosing names that begin with an underscore as the C libraries use that naming convention.

Hot tip

Whitespace is ignored by the C compiler but program code should always end with a newline (press Return).

hello.c

The program code begins with an instruction to the C compiler to include information from the standard input/output library, stdio.h. This makes the functions within that library available for use in this program. One of these is a function named printf() that is used to write the output from a program.

The instruction is more properly called a "preprocessor" instruction and must be placed at the start of the page, before the actual program code is processed. The # hash character starts the line to denote a preprocessor instruction. Notice that the name of the library file must be enclosed by < and > angled brackets.

In the function declaration the data-type is specified as int, meaning integer. This means that after executing its statements this function must return an integer value to the operating system.

As this program contains just one function it must be named as the obligatory main() function that is required in all C programs. The plain brackets after the main() function-name are empty as no optional arguments have been specified.

The braces contain the statements to be executed by the program. The first statement calls upon the printf() function that is defined in the standard input/output library. It specifies as its argument a string of text inside double quotes. In C programming, strings must always be enclosed in double quotes.

This string contains the text "Hello World" and the newline escape sequence \n. This is one of the escape sequences listed in the Handy Reference on the inner front cover of this book. It will move the print head to the left margin of the next line following output of the "Hello World" text.

The second and final statement in the main() function uses the C keyword return to return a value of zero to the operating system. Traditionally returning a zero value after the execution of a program indicates to the operating system that the program executed correctly.

The program in text format is saved with the ".c" file extension as hello.c and is ready to be compiled to create an executable version in machine-readable byte code format.

Don't forget

Each statement must be terminated with a semi-colon.

13

Compiling and running

The C source code files for the examples in this book are stored in a directory created expressly for that purpose. The directory is named "MyPrograms" and its absolute address on Windows is C:\MyPrograms, whereas on Linux it's at /home/MyPrograms.

The hello.c program source code file, created on the previous page, is saved in this directory awaiting compilation to produce a version in executable byte code format.

From a command prompt navigate to the MyPrograms directory, then type gcc hello.c to attempt to compile the C program. When the attempt succeeds the compiler creates an executable file alongside the original source code file. By default this file will be called a.out on Linux systems and a.exe on Windows systems.

Compiling a different C source code file in the MyPrograms directory would now overwrite the first executable file without warning. This is obviously unsatisfactory so a custom name for the executable file must be specified when compiling hello.c.

To make the compiler generate an executable file with a specific name use its -o option, followed by your preferred file name.

On either Windows or Linux platforms now type the command gcc hello.c -o hello.exe at a prompt in the MyPrograms directory. This will compile the hello.c source code file and generate an executable file named hello.exe.

Hot tip

At a command prompt type gcc --help to see a list of all the possible compiler options.

14

Don't forget

If the compiler complains that there is no newline at the end of the file add a carriage return to the end of the source code and retry.

To run the generated executable program file in Windows simply type the file name hello.exe at the command prompt in the MyPrograms directory.

Because Linux does not, by default, look in the current directory for executable files, unless it is specifically directed to do so, it is necessary to prefix the file name with ./ to execute the program.

Hot tip

Windows users can even omit the file extension to run programs. In this case, just typing hello is sufficient.

Adding comments

It is good programming practice to add comments to your C source code. This makes the code more easily understood when read by other people, or by yourself when revisiting a piece of code after a period of absence.

Any remarks that appear between /* and */ are ignored by the C compiler, even when spread across multiple lines on the page.

Most commercial C programs begin with a comment block describing the purpose of the program together with other information such as the author's name, date the program was written, copyright permissions, etc..

Comments may also describe the purpose of individual functions and statements. The previous program hello.c, listed on page 12, could be enhanced with useful comments like those below:

hello.c
(commented)

```
/*
    This is a first program to introduce C programming.
    Its purpose is to generate the traditional message
    of "Hello World", then move on to a new line.
*/


/*
    First make the standard input/output functions
    in the stdio.h header available to this program.
*/

#include <stdio.h>


/* declare the obligatory main() function */

int main()
{

  /* call the printf() function to output a string */

  printf("Hello World\n");

  /* return zero to confirm that the program ran OK */

  return 0;

}
```

Don't forget

This is ideally how C source code should be commented – the examples in this book are largely uncommented, however, because of space limitations.

2 Storing data

This chapter introduces the "variable" object and demonstrates how it may be used to store dynamic data in a C program.

Creating variables

A variable is like a container in a C program in which a data value can be stored inside the computer's memory. The stored value can be referenced using the variable's name. The programmer can choose any name for a variable providing it follows the naming conventions listed in the table below:

Naming rule	Example
CANNOT contain any of the C keywords	volatile
CANNOT contain arithmetic operators	a+b*c
CANNOT contain punctuation characters	%$#@!
CANNOT contain any spaces	no spaces
CANNOT start with a number	2bad
CAN contain numbers elsewhere	good1
CAN contain mixed case	UPdown
CAN contain underscores	_is_good

Beware

Variable names are case-sensitive in C – so variables named "VAR", "Var" and "var" would be treated as three separate variables by the program.

18

Don't forget

C keywords are listed in a table on the inner front cover of this book.

It is good practice to choose meaningful names for variables to make the program more easily understood. To create a variable in a program requires it to be "declared". A variable declaration has this syntax:

data-type variable-name ;

First the declaration specifies which type of data the variable is permitted to contain. This will be one of the four data types described on the opposite page. The type is followed by a space then the chosen variable name, adhering to the naming rules. Finally the declaration is terminated by a semi-colon. This is used much like a full stop in the English language to mark the end of a sentence. Multiple variables of the same data type can be created in a single declaration by separating their names with a comma:

data-type variable1 , variable2 , variable3 ;

There are four basic data types in the C language. These are defined using the C keywords which are listed in the following table, together with a description of each data type:

Data type	Description	Example
char	A single byte, capable of holding one character	A
int	An integer whole number	100
float	A floating-point number, correct to six decimal places	0.123456
double	A floating-point number, correct to ten decimal places	0.0123456789

The four data types allocate different amounts of machine memory for storing data. The smallest is the char data type, which allocates just a single byte of memory, and the largest is the double data type. The double data type allocates twice the amount of memory that the float data type does, so it should only be used when a lengthy precise floating point number is a necessity.

Variable declarations should be made before any executable code appears in a program. When a value is assigned to a variable that variable is said to have been "initialized". Optionally a variable may be initialized when it is declared.

The example code fragment below creates a variety of variables and initializes them with appropriate values:

```
int num1, num2;        /* declare 2 int variables */
char letter;           /* declare a char variable */
float decimal = 7.5;   /* declare and initialize a
                               float variable */

num1 = 100;      /* initialize the int variables */
num2 = 200;

letter = 'A';    /* initialize the char variable */
```

Beware

Values of the char data type must always be enclosed by single quotes – double quotes are incorrect.

Displaying variable values

The value of variables can be displayed using the printf() function that was used in chapter 1 to display the "Hello World" message. The desired format in which to display the variable value must be specified as an argument in the printf() function's parentheses using a suitable "format specifier", along with the variable name:

Format specifier	Description	Example
%d	An integer whole number	100
%f	A floating-point number	0.123456
%c	A single character	'A'
%s	A string of characters	"Hello World"
%p	A machine memory address	0x0022FF5C

Don't forget

Single char characters must be enclosed by single quotes – a string of characters, on the other hand, must be enclosed by double quotes.

The example program code below demonstrates the declaration of a variable of the double data type. It is initialized, with an appropriate value, then its value displayed in the program output.

```c
#include <stdio.h>

int main()
{
    double pi = 3.1415926536;
    printf("The value of pi is approximately %f", pi );
    return 0;
}
```

firstvar.c

Hot tip

Here the double value is rounded up to fit the default %f format size of just six decimal places – use %.10f to display all ten decimal places.

```
C:\MyPrograms>gcc firstvar.c -o firstvar.exe

C:\MyPrograms>firstvar
The value of pi is approximately 3.141593
C:\MyPrograms>
```

Inputting variable values

The "scanf()" function can be used to get input into a program and it requires two arguments. First a format specifier defines the type of data to be entered, then the name of the a variable in which the input will be stored. The variable name must be preceded by a "&" character, except when the data being entered is a string of text. The & character, in this case, is the "addressof" operator that directs the input to be stored in the variable name that it precedes.

The scanf() function can set the value of multiple variables simultaneously too. The first argument must then contain a list of required format specifiers, each separated by a space, and the entire list should be enclosed by double quotes. The second argument must contain a comma-separated list of variable names to which each specified format applies.

In the following example, the program requests data to be entered which is then assigned to three variables by the scanf() function.

```c
#include <stdio.h>

int main()
{
    char character; int a,b;
    printf("Enter any one keyboard character: ");
    scanf( "%c", &character );
    printf("Enter 2 integers separated by a space: ");
    scanf( "%d %d", &a, &b );
    printf("The letter entered was %c\n", character);
    printf("Integers entered were %d and %d\n", a, b);
    return 0;
}
```

Hot tip

Strings are a special case and are demonstrated with the topic of arrays, on page 30.

setvars.c

```
C:\MyPrograms>gcc setvars.c -o setvars.exe

C:\MyPrograms>setvars
Enter any one keyboard character: m
Enter 2 integers separated by a space: 100 200
The letter entered was m
Integers entered were 100 and 200

C:\MyPrograms>
```

Beware

Note that the scanf() function stops reading input when it encounters a blank space.

Formatting output

The format specifiers listed in the table on page 20 can be used to control how output appears. A program can ensure that output occupies a specific minimum number of spaces by specifying the required number in the format specifier. The number must be placed immediately after the % character in the format specifier.

For instance, to ensure that an integer always fills at least 7 spaces the format specifier is %7d.

If it is preferable for the blank spaces to be filled with zeros just add a zero between the % character and the specified number. To ensure that an integer always fills at least 7 spaces, and that any blank spaces are filled with zeros, the format specifier is %07d.

spaces.c

```
#include <stdio.h>

int main()
{
  int num = 1;
  printf("Using %%0d  displays %0d\n", num);
  printf("Using %%1d  displays %1d\n", num);
  printf("Using %%2d  displays %2d\n", num);
  printf("Using %%3d  displays %3d\n", num);
  printf("Using %%4d  displays %4d\n", num);
  printf("Using %%05d displays %05d\n", num);
  printf("Using %%06d displays %06d\n", num);
  printf("Using %%07d displays %07d\n", num);
  return 0;
}
```

Don't forget

To display a "%" character with the printf() function prefix it with another "%" character – as seen here.

Hot tip

This example adds blank and zero-filled spaces to the output – only if the number stated in the format specifier is greater than the number of spaces occupied by the integer.

```
C:\MyPrograms>gcc spaces.c -o spaces.exe

C:\MyPrograms>spaces
Using %0d  displays 1
Using %1d  displays 1
Using %2d  displays  1
Using %3d  displays   1
Using %4d  displays    1
Using %05d displays 00001
Using %06d displays 000001
Using %07d displays 0000001

C:\MyPrograms>
```

Greater control over the output appearance of floating-point numbers can be gained by adding a "precision specifier" to the %f format specifier. This is simply a full stop followed by a number representing the desired number of decimal places to be displayed. For instance, a format specifier of %.2f will display a floating-point number showing just 2 decimal places.

The minimum space specifier, described on the opposite page, can be combined with the precision specifier so that both number of minimum spaces and number of decimal places can be controlled. For instance, a format specifier of %07.2f would display seven spaces, with two decimal places, and any empty spaces would be filled with zeros.

By default, any empty spaces precede the number so it is right-aligned. To have the number displayed left-aligned, with any empty spaces added after the number, prefix the minimum space specifier with a minus sign, as in the example below. The "end" strings are just there to show that empty spaces have been added.

```
#include <stdio.h>

int main()
{
    float num = 7.123456;
    printf("%-8.0f end\n", num);
    printf("%-8.2f end\n", num);
    printf("%-8.4f end\n", num);
    printf("%-8.6f end\n", num);
    return 0;
}
```

precision.c

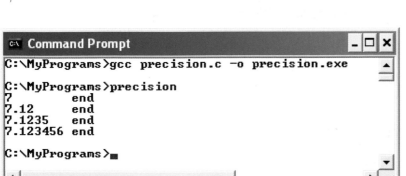

```
Command Prompt                                    - □ ×
C:\MyPrograms>gcc precision.c -o precision.exe

C:\MyPrograms>precision
7          end
7.12       end
7.1235     end
7.123456 end

C:\MyPrograms>
```

Don't forget

The decimal places may be rounded – in this example the number to 4 decimal places has been rounded up to 7.1235.

Data type qualifiers

When an int variable is declared it can by default contain either positive of negative integer values. These are known as "signed" values. The range of possible values is determined by your system.

If the int variable is created by default as a "long" type it typically will have a possible range of values from a maximum of +2147483647 down to a minimum of -2147483648.

On the other hand, if the int variable is created by default as a "short" type then typically the maximum possible value will be +32767 and its minimum will be -32768.

The size can be specified when declaring the variable using the short and long keywords, as demonstrated in this code fragment:

```
short int num1;          /* saves memory space */

long int num2;           /* allows bigger range */
```

The limits.h header file contains implementation-defined limits for the size of each data type. These are accessed via "constant" values called INT_MAX and INT_MIN, for int variable declarations of unspecified size. Similarly, SHRT_MAX and SHRT_MIN for short int variable declarations and LONG_MIN and LONG_MAX for long int variable declarations.

The code below displays each of these ranges, shown in the illustration at the top of the opposite page:

```
#include <stdio.h>

#include <limits.h>

int main()
{
    printf("Max int: %d\t",    INT_MAX );
    printf("Min int: %d\n",    INT_MIN );
    printf("Max short: %d\t", SHRT_MAX );
    printf("Min short: %d\n", SHRT_MIN );
    printf("Max long: %d\t",  LONG_MAX );
    printf("Min long: %d\n",  LONG_MIN );
    return 0;
}
```

Hot tip

Constant values are always referred to in uppercase to distinguish them from variable values.

maxmin.c

Don't forget

The code must first include the limits.h header file in order to have access to its features.

24

A non-negative "unsigned" int can be declared with the unsigned keyword. An unsigned short int variable will typically have a possible range from 0 to 65,535. An unsigned long int variable will typically have a possible range from 0 to 4,294,967,295.

The sizeof operator is used in this example to examine the amount of memory space allocated to various data types:

```c
#include <stdio.h>
int main()
{
  printf("short int: %d bytes\t",sizeof(short int));
  printf("long int: %d bytes\n", sizeof(long int));
  printf("unsigned long int: %d bytes\n",
                       sizeof(unsigned long int));

  printf("char: %d byte\t",sizeof(char));
  printf("float: %d bytes\t",sizeof(float));
  printf("double: %d bytes\t\n", sizeof(double));
  return 0;
}
```

sizeof.c

Hot tip

Notice how the \t escape sequence formats output.

Don't forget

The default size of memory space allocated to a variable is system-dependent.

25

External variables

The extent to which a variable is accessible in a program is called the "variable scope". Variables declared internally inside a function are known as "local" variables, whereas variables that are declared externally outside of a function are known as "global" variables.

Local variables can only be accessed by the function in which they are declared. They come into existence when the function is called and normally disappear when the function is exited.

Global variables, on the other hand, can be accessed by all functions in a program. They remain in existence permanently so are useful to communicate data between functions.

An external global variable must be defined exactly once at the start of the program. It must also be declared at the start of each function that wants to use it. Each declaration should begin with the extern keyword which denotes that it is for a global variable, rather than for a regular local variable. These declarations should not be used to initialize the global variable.

The example below demonstrates how to define , declare and initialize an external global variable called "num":

Hot tip

The true value of external variables is more apparent in programs that have multiple functions.

26

extvars.c

```c
#include <stdio.h>

int num;              /* define an external variable */

int main()
{
  extern int num;  /* declare the external variable */
  num = 5;         /* initialize the external variable */
  printf("Global variable value is %d", num);
  return 0;
}
```

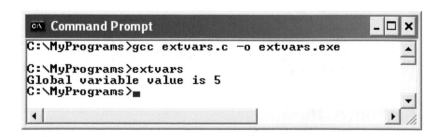

Static variables

Larger C programs consist of multiple source code files that are compiled together to create a final executable file. This is a very useful aspect of C programming that allows source code to be modular so that it can be reused in different programs.

Global external variables, as described on the opposite page, would normally be accessible to any function in any of the files being compiled together. All functions are normally accessible globally too. Functions and, more usually, external variables can have their accessibility limited to just the file in which they are created by the use of the static keyword.

Normally a program cannot employ more than one variable of any given name. Using static external variables, however, usefully allows external variables of the same name to coexist happily providing they are declared as static and are not in the same file. Programming with multiple source code files can find a common external variable name duplicated in two files. Declaring these as static avoids the need to rename one of these variables in each occurrence within the source code.

The example below creates a static global external variable that cannot be used by other source code files. Attempting to do so causes an error at compile-time and the compilation will halt.

```c
#include <stdio.h>

/* define and initialize a static external variable */
static int num = 100;

int main()
{
   extern int num;   /* declare the external variable */
   printf("Global value: %d", num);
}
```

Hot tip

Internal variables can also be declared as static – these are only accessible by the function in which they are declared but they do not disappear when the function is exited. This offers permanent private storage within a function.

static.c

27

```
 Command Prompt                          – □ ✗

C:\MyPrograms>gcc static.c -o static.exe

C:\MyPrograms>static
Global value: 100
C:\MyPrograms>_
```

Register variables

A register variable declaration informs the compiler that the specified variable will be heavily-used by the program. The intention is for the compiler to place register variables in the machine registers of the computer to speed access times. Their usefulness may be questionable though as compilers are free to ignore this advice.

Only local internal variables can be declared as register variables. In any case only a few variables can be kept in registers and they may only be of certain types. The precise limitations vary from machine to machine.

Despite these possible drawbacks register declarations are harmless because the register keyword is ignored when the compiler cannot actually use machine registers to store the variable. Instead, the variable is created as though the register keyword was not there.

One sort of variable that might benefit from being a register variable is that used to store the control value of a loop. On each iteration of the loop that variable value must be compared and changed so the variable is being repeatedly accessed. Loops are covered in chapter 5, but the loop example below is included here to illustrate the repeated access of an intended register variable.

28

Hot tip

A variable declared with the "volatile" keyword is not allowed to be stored in a machine register – this is the opposite effect to a register variable.

register.c

```c
#include <stdio.h>
int main()
{
    register int num = 0;

    while( num < 5)
    { ++num; printf(" Pass %d |", num); }
    return 0;
}
```

Hot tip

Here the loop adds 1 to the variable value while it remains below 5 and outputs a text string showing its current value on each iteration.

```
Command Prompt                                    _ □ ✕
C:\MyPrograms>gcc register.c -o register.exe

C:\MyPrograms>register
 Pass 1 | Pass 2 | Pass 3 | Pass 4 | Pass 5 |
C:\MyPrograms>
```

Converting data types

Any data stored in a variable can be forced (coerced) into a variable of a different data type by a process known as "casting". A cast just states the data type to which the value should be converted in plain brackets before its variable name, like this:

variable-name = (*data-type*) *variable-name* ;

The example below casts both float and char values into int type variables:

```c
#include <stdio.h>
int main()
{
   int num1, num2;          /* declare int variables */
   float dec;               /* declare a float variable */
   char letter;             /* declare a char variable */

   dec = 7.5;          /* initialize the float variable */
   letter = 'A';       /* initialize the char variable */

   num1 = (int) dec;       /* cast float into an int */
   num2 = (int) letter;    /* cast char into an int */

   printf("num1 is: %d\n",num1);
   printf("num2 is: %d\n",num2);
   return 0;
}
```

cast.c

Hot tip

Note that the float value in this example is simply truncated when cast into the int variable – it is not rounded.

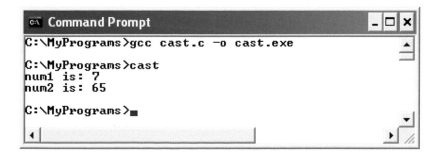

```
Command Prompt                          _ □ ×
C:\MyPrograms>gcc cast.c -o cast.exe

C:\MyPrograms>cast
num1 is: 7
num2 is: 65

C:\MyPrograms>
```

Hot tip

ASCII" (pronounced "as-kee") stands for "American Standard Code for Information Interchange" and is the accepted standard for plain text. You can see the full range of standard ASCII codes on pages 162 and 163.

Characters are represented by a numerical ASCII code within the range of 0 - 127. The uppercase letter 'A' in this example is represented by the ASCII numerical code of 65, so that is its integer value when cast into an int type variable.

Arrays

An array is a variable that can store multiple items of data, unlike a regular variable which can only store a single item of data.

The pieces of data are stored sequentially in array "elements" that are numbered, starting at zero. So the first array value is stored in array element zero, the second array value is stored in array element 1, and so on.

An array is declared in a C program in the same way as regular variables but additionally the size of the array should be specified in the declaration. This should be stated in square brackets following the array name, with this syntax:

data-type array-name [number-of-elements] ;

Optionally, an array can be initialized when it is declared by assigning values to each element as a comma-separated list enclosed by curly brackets (braces).

Individual elements can be referenced using the array name followed by square brackets containing the element number.

This example creates an array of three elements and assigns initial values to them. The second element is then changed before each value is displayed in the program output.

```c
#include <stdio.h>

int main()
{
  /* create an integer array with three elements */
  int arr[3] = { 10, 2, 8 };

  /* change the value of the array's second element */
  arr[1] = 9;

  /* display the value stored inside each element */
  printf("element 0 contains %d\n", arr[0] );
  printf("element 1 contains %d\n", arr[1] );
  printf("element 2 contains %d\n", arr[2] );

  return 0;

}
```

Hot tip

It is acceptable to omit the number from the square brackets (to create an unsized array) if the elements are being initialized in the array declaration – the size will be adjusted automatically to fit the number of elements assigned to that array.

array.c

Don't forget

Array elements start numbering at zero, not one.

One of the most significant uses of arrays in C programming concerns their ability to store strings of text. Each element in an array of the char data type can store a single character. Adding the special \0 null character escape sequence in the array's final element promotes the array to string status.

An entire string can be referenced using just the array name and can be displayed using the %s format specifier.

The example below creates an array with five elements – to contain a four-letter string plus the \0 null character string terminator. This entire string is then output by the program.

Don't forget

When creating an array to hold a string remember to allow space for an element at the end to contain the null character.

31

```c
#include <stdio.h>

int main()
{
    char arr[5] = { 'm', 'i', 'k', 'e', '\0' };

    printf("The array contains the string %s\n", arr );

    return 0;

}
```

string.c

Multi-dimensional arrays

An array can have more than one index – to represent multiple dimensions, rather than the single dimension of a regular array.

Multi-dimensional arrays of three indices and more are uncommon, but 2-dimensional arrays are useful to store grid-based information such as coordinates.

The following example creates a 2-dimensional array where the first index has two elements and the second index has three. This represents a table of two rows and three columns – here the first row contains characters and the second row contains numbers.

Notice the arrangement of the braces to assign initial values to each element of the indices in the array declaration.

array2d.c

```c
#include <stdio.h>

int main()
{
    int arr[2][3] = { {'A', 'B', 'C' } , { 1, 2, 3 } };

    printf("array [0][0] contains %c\n", arr[0][0] );
    printf("array [0][1] contains %c\n", arr[0][1] );
    printf("array [0][2] contains %c\n", arr[0][2] );

    printf("array [1][0] contains %d\n", arr[1][0] );
    printf("array [1][1] contains %d\n", arr[1][1] );
    printf("array [1][2] contains %d\n", arr[1][2] );

    return 0;
}
```

32

Hot tip

Note that the assigned characters in this example are stored as their ASCII integer value then converted back to characters for display by the %c format specifier.

```
C:\MyPrograms>gcc array2d.c -o array2d.exe

C:\MyPrograms>array2d
array [0][0] contains A
array [0][1] contains B
array [0][2] contains C
array [1][0] contains 1
array [1][1] contains 2
array [1][2] contains 3

C:\MyPrograms>
```

Setting constant values

This chapter introduces the "constant" object and demonstrates how it may be used to store fixed data in a C program.

Declaring constants

A constant can be declared in the same way as a variable but preceded by the const keyword. It should be initialized by assigning its permanent value in the declaration. The program may not subsequently assign a different value to the constant.

The example program below calculates the area and circumference of a circle from a diameter value supplied by the user. Both calculations use Pi. The value of Pi will not change so can usefully be assigned to a constant. Notice that it is convention to use uppercase characters for constant names, to readily distinguish them from variable names in the program code.

const.c

```c
#include <stdio.h>

int main()
{
    const float PI = 3.141593;
    int diameter;
    float radius, circ, area;

    printf("\nEnter the diameter of a ");
    printf("circle in millimeters:");
    scanf("%d", &diameter);

    circ =   (float) PI * diameter;
    radius = (float) diameter / 2;
    area =   (float) PI * (radius * radius);

    printf("\tIts circumference is %.2f mm\n", circ);
    printf("\tAnd its area is %.2f sq.mm\n", area);
    return 0;
}
```

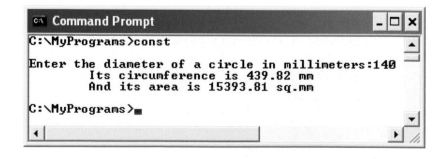

```
Command Prompt                                      _ □ ✕

C:\MyPrograms>const

Enter the diameter of a circle in millimeters:140
        Its circumference is 439.82 mm
        And its area is 15393.81 sq.mm

C:\MyPrograms>_
```

Enumerating constants

The enum keyword provides a handy way to create a sequence of integer constants in a concise manner. Optionally the declaration can include a name for the sequence after the enum keyword. The constant names follow as a comma-separated list within braces.

Each of the constants will by default have a value 1 greater than the constant that it follows in the list. Unless specified the first constant will have a value of zero, the next a value of 1, and so on.

The constants can be assigned any individual value but the following constants will always increment it one by one.

This example represents the points value of balls in the game of snooker starting at 1 for the red ball, right up to 7 for the black ball.

The sequence is named "colors" but this could have been omitted.

```c
#include <stdio.h>

int main()
{
  enum colors
    { RED = 1,YELLOW,GREEN,BROWN,BLUE,PINK,BLACK };
  int total;

  printf("I potted a red worth %d\n", RED );
  printf("Then a black worth %d\n", BLACK );
  printf("Followed by another red worth %d\n", RED );
  total = RED + BLACK + RED;
  printf("Altogether I scored %d\n", total);
  return 0;
}
```

enum.c

```
C:\MyPrograms>gcc enum.c -o enum.exe

C:\MyPrograms>enum
I potted a red worth 1
Then a black worth 7
Followed by another red worth 1
Altogether I scored 9

C:\MyPrograms>
```

Don't forget

Assigning a value of 1 to the BLUE constant in this example would automatically make the PINK constant 2 and the BLACK constant 3.

Creating a constant type

Once an enumerated sequence has been declared it can be considered as a new data type in its own right with properties of its specified constant names, and their associated values.

Variables of this data type can be declared like any other variable using the syntax:

data-type variable-name ;

The example below builds on the previous example which created a data-type called colors. A new variable of that type is declared with the name of "fingers". This variable can be assigned any of the constant names specified in the colors enumeration list. In this case it is assigned the sum of the PINK (6) and BROWN (4) constant values:

enumtypes.c

Beware

The addition of PINK and BROWN values (6+4) returns an int data type (10). So the cast is essential to assign this value to the fingers variable – which is an enum colors data type, not an int type.

```c
#include <stdio.h>

int main()
{
  /* declare a sequence of constants */
  enum colors
  { RED = 1, YELLOW,GREEN,BROWN,BLUE,PINK,BLACK };

  /* declare a variable of the enumerated data type */
  enum colors fingers;

  /* assign valid constants from the colors list */
  fingers = (enum colors) PINK + BROWN;

  /* display the value in the variable */
  printf("value: %d\n", fingers);

  return 0;
}
```

```
C:\ Command Prompt                           _ □ ✕

C:\MyPrograms>gcc enumtypes.c -o enumtypes.exe

C:\MyPrograms>enumtypes
value: 10

C:\MyPrograms>_
```

Custom data types can be defined using the typedef keyword. A custom type declaration has this syntax:

typedef definition type-name ;

The creation of two custom data types is illustrated in the following example. The first is a data type called COLORS of the enum colors type from the previous example. The second is a data type called USHRT of the unsigned short int type. Declaring custom data types can make program code more concise.

```c
#include <stdio.h>

/* declare a sequence of constants */
enum colors
    { RED =1, YELLOW,GREEN,BROWN,BLUE,PINK,BLACK };

/* declare a custom type, of the enum colors type */
typedef enum colors COLORS;

/* declare a custom unsigned short int type */
typedef unsigned short int USHRT;

int main()
{
  /* declare variables of the custom data types */
  USHRT num = 16;
  COLORS fingers = (COLORS) BROWN + PINK;

  /* display the variable values */
  printf("values: %d %d\n", fingers, num);

  return 0;
}
```

typedef.c

Don't forget

Custom data types must be declared in the program before variables of that type can be created – write the declarations before the main() function to ensure those types will be available, as in this example.

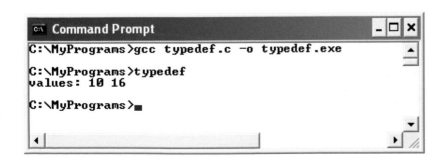

```
C:\MyPrograms>gcc typedef.c -o typedef.exe

C:\MyPrograms>typedef
values: 10 16

C:\MyPrograms>
```

37

Defining constants

The preprocessor directive #define can be used to specify constant text values that can be used in the program with this syntax:

#define CONSTANT-NAME "text-string"

Like the #include directive, these should appear at the very start of the program code. Any occurrences of the specified constant name in the program code has its associated text string substituted by the compiler before the program is compiled.

The example below defines three string constants with #define preprocessor directives and their specified constant names are used in the calls to the printf() function. When this program is compiled the compiler first substitutes the text strings in place of the constant names.

Defining text string constants in this way makes the program code much neater and, therefore, more readable.

Hot tip

The #define directives are also known as "macro definitions".

define.c

```
#include <stdio.h>
#define LINE "_____"
#define TITLE "C Programming in easy steps"
#define AUTHOR "Mike McGrath"

int main()
{
  printf("\n \t %s \n \t %s \n", LINE, TITLE );
  printf("\t by %s \n \t %s \n ", AUTHOR, LINE );
  return 0;
}
```

Hot tip

The LINE string in this example is just a series of underscore characters.

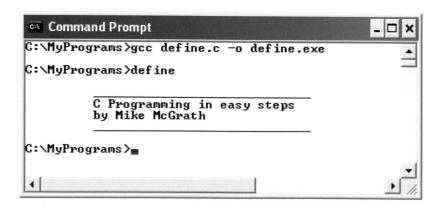

Command Prompt

```
C:\MyPrograms>gcc define.c -o define.exe

C:\MyPrograms>define


        _____
        C Programming in easy steps
        by Mike McGrath
        _____

C:\MyPrograms>
```

38

Conditional definitions

A preprocessor "macro" can define a constant according to the result of an #if directive test to evaluate an expression. Depending upon the result of this test the macro could then #define a constant. The macro must end with an #endif directive.

The existence of a constant definition can be tested for with an #ifdef directive. This is used in the following example to test for the existence of system constants that are defined by the C compiler itself. A custom constant called SYS is then defined as a text string appropriate to the host operating system.

```c
#include <stdio.h>
#ifdef _WIN32
 #define SYS "Windows"
#endif
#ifdef linux
 #define SYS "Linux"
#endif

int main()
{
  printf("Operating system: %s\n", SYS );
  return 0;
}
```

ifmacro.c

```
C:\MyPrograms>gcc ifmacro.c -o ifmacro.exe

C:\MyPrograms>ifmacro
Operating system: Windows
```

Compiler-defined constants vary from machine to machine. To discover those on your own system type cpp -dM file.c at a prompt, where file.c is a valid C file to be compiled. A list of constants will be written out to the screen.

```
user> gcc ifmacro.c -o ifmacro.exe
user> ./ifmacro.exe
Operating system Linux
user>
```

Debugging definitions

Alternatives in an #if directive test can be offered with #else and #elif (else if) directives. This allows conditional branching of the program to run sections of the code according to the test result.

Constants defined with a #define directive can be undefined with the #undef directive. The #ifdef directive, introduced on the previous page, has a companion directive #ifndef (if not defined). This can be useful when debugging problem code to hide and unhide sections of the program.

All these preprocessor directives are demonstrated in this example:

debug.c

```c
#include <stdio.h>
#define DEBUG 2

int main()
{
  #if DEBUG == 1
    printf("Debug Status is 1\n");
  #elif DEBUG == 2
    printf("Debug Status is 2\n");
  #else
    printf("Default Debug Status\n");
  #endif

  #undef DEBUG

  #ifndef DEBUG
    printf("Debug Status is OFF\n");
  #endif

  return 0;
}
```

Hot tip

The "==" equality operator in this example means "is equal to".

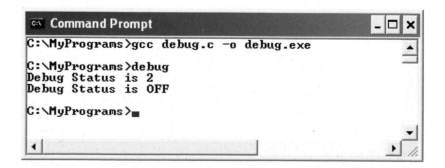

```
Command Prompt                          - □ ×
C:\MyPrograms>gcc debug.c -o debug.exe

C:\MyPrograms>debug
Debug Status is 2
Debug Status is OFF

C:\MyPrograms>_
```

Performing operations

This chapter introduces the common "operators" and demonstrates how they may be used to manipulate data in a C program.

Arithmetical operators

The arithmetical operators commonly used in C programs are listed in the table below together with the operation they perform:

Operator	Operation
+	Addition
–	Subtraction
*	Multiplication
/	Division
%	Modulus
++	Increment
– –	Decrement

Hot tip

The numbers used along with operators to form expressions are called "operands" – in the expression "2+3" the numbers 2 and 3 are the operands.

The operators for addition, subtraction, multiplication and division act as you would expect. Care must be taken, however, to bracket expressions for clarity where more than one operators is used:

```
a = b * c - d % e / f ;          /* this is unclear */

a = (b * c) - ((d % e) / f ) ;   /* this is clearer */
```

The % modulus operator will divide the first given number by the second given number and return the remainder of the operation. This is useful to determine if a number has an odd or even value.

The ++ increment operator and – – decrement operator alter the given value by 1 and return the resulting new value. These are most commonly used to count iterations in a loop. The ++ increment operator increases the value by one while the – – decrement operator decreases the value by one.

The increment and decrement operators can be placed before or after a value, to different effect. If placed before the operand (prefix), its value is immediately changed, if placed after the operand (postfix) its value is noted first, then the value is changed.

The difference between placing the increment operator before and after an int variable operand is demonstrated in this example which illustrates each of the arithmetical operators in action:

```c
#include <stdio.h>
int main()
{
    int a = 4, b = 8, c = 1, d = 1, result;

    result = a + b;
    printf("Added numbers total %d\n",result);
    result = b - a;
    printf("Subtracted numbers total %d\n",result);
    result = a * b;
    printf("Multiplied numbers total %d\n",result);
    result = b / a;
    printf("Divided numbers total %d\n",result);
    result = a % b;
    printf("Modulus of numbers is %d\n",result);

    printf("Postfix increment is %d\n", c++);
    printf("Now postfix increment is %d\n", c);
    printf("Prefix increment is %d\n",++d);
    printf("Now prefix increment is %d\n",d);

    return 0;
}
```

arithmetic.c

Hot tip

Notice that the variable value is immediately increased only with the prefix increment operator.

43

```
Command Prompt                          _ □ ✕
C:\MyPrograms>gcc arithmetic.c -o arithmetic.exe

C:\MyPrograms>arithmetic
Added numbers total 12
Subtracted numbers total 4
Multiplied numbers total 32
Divided numbers total 2
Modulus of numbers is 4
Postfix increment is 1
Now postfix increment is 2
Prefix increment is 2
Now prefix increment is 2

C:\MyPrograms>_
```

Logical operators

The logical operators most commonly used in C programs are listed in the table below:

Operator	Operation
&&	Logical AND
||	Logical OR
!	Logical NOT

The logical operators are used with operands that have the boolean values of true or false, or are values that can convert to true or false.

The logical && AND operator will evaluate two operands and return true only if both operands themselves are true. Otherwise the && operator will return false.

This is used in conditional branching where the direction of a C program is determined by testing two conditions. If both conditions are satisfied the program will go in a certain direction, otherwise it will take a different direction.

Unlike the && operator that needs both operands to be true the || OR operator will evaluate its two operands and return true if either one of the operands itself returns true. If neither operand returns true then || will return false. This is useful in C programming to perform a certain action if either one of two test conditions has been met.

The third logical operator ! NOT is a unary operator that is used before a single operand. It returns the inverse value of the given operand so if the variable a had a value of true then !a would have a value of false. The ! operator is useful in C programs to toggle the value of a variable in successive loop iterations with a statement like a=!a. This ensures that on each pass the value is changed, like flicking a light switch on and off.

In C programming a zero represents the boolean false value and any non-zero value, such as 1, represents the boolean true value.

Hot tip

The term "boolean" refers to a system of logical thought developed by the English mathematician George Boole (1815-64).

The example below demonstrates how boolean values can be tested with each of the logical operators shown opposite. The ! NOT operator reverses the boolean value, && AND returns 1 if both operands are non-zero values and || OR returns 1 if either operand is a non-zero value.

```c
#include <stdio.h>
int main()
{
  int a = 1, b = 0;

  printf("AND examples:\n");
  printf("\t a && a = %d (true)\n",  a && a );
  printf("\t a && b = %d (false)\n", a && b );
  printf("\t b && b = %d (false)\n", b && b );

  printf("OR examples:\n");
  printf("\t a || a = %d (true)\n",  a || a );
  printf("\t a || b = %d (true)\n",  a || b );
  printf("\t b || b = %d (false)\n", b || b );

  printf("NOT examples:\n");
  printf("\ta = %d !a = %d\n", a, !a );
  printf("\tb = %d !b = %d\n", b, !b );
  return 0;
}
```

logic.c

Hot tip

Notice that 0 && 0 returns 0, not 1 – demonstrating the anecdote "two wrongs don't make a right".

Assignment operators

The operators that are used in C programming to assign values are listed in the table below. All except the simple = assign operator are a shorthand form of a longer expression so each equivalent is also given for clarity.

Operator	Example	Equivalent
=	a = b	a = b
+=	a += b	a = (a + b)
-=	a -= b	a = (a - b)
*=	a *= b	a = (a * b)
/=	a /= b	a = (a / b)
%=	a %= b	a = (a % b)

It is important to regard the = operator to mean "assign" rather than "equals" to avoid confusion with the == equality operator.

In the example above the variable named a is assigned the value that is contained in the variable named b – so that becomes the new value stored in the a variable.

The += operator is useful to add a value onto an existing value that is stored in a variable. In the table example the += operator first adds the value contained in variable a to the value contained in the variable named b. It then assigns the result to become the new value stored in the a variable.

All the other operators in the table work in the same way by making the arithmetical operation between the two values first, then assigning the result to the first variable to become its new stored value.

With the %= operator the first operand a is divided by the second operand b then the remainder of the operation is assigned to the a variable.

Beware

The == equality operator compares operand values and is described on page 48.

The example program below performs a series of operations to demonstrate each of the assignment operators in action:

```c
#include <stdio.h>
int main()
{
  int a, b;

  printf("Assign values example:\n");
  printf("\tVariable a = %d\n", a = 8 );
  printf("\tVariable b = %d\n", b = 4 );

  printf("Add & assign example:\n");
  printf("\tVariable a += b;(8+=4) a = %d\n",a += b);
  printf("Subtract & assign example:\n");
  printf("\tVariable a -= b;(12-=4) a = %d\n",a -= b);
  printf("Multiply & assign example:\n");
  printf("\tVariable a *= b;(8*=4)  a = %d\n",a *= b);
  printf("Divide & assign example:\n");
  printf("\tVariable a /= b;(32/=4) a = %d\n",a /= b);
  printf("Modulus & assign example:\n\t");
  printf("Variable a %%- b;(8%%4)  a = %d\n",a %= b);

  return 0;
}
```

assign.c

47

Hot tip

Notice that %% must be used in order to display the % character with the printf() function.

Comparison operators

The operators that are commonly used in C programming to compare two numerical values are listed in the table below:

Operator	Comparative test
==	Equality
!=	Inequality
>	Greater than
<	Less than
>=	Greater than or equal to
<=	Less than or equal to

Hot tip

Further information on ASCII codes can be found in the Reference section on pages 162 and 163.

The == equality operator compares two operands and will return 1 (true) if both are equal in value, otherwise it will return 0 (false). If both are the same number they are equal, or if both are characters their ASCII code value is compared numerically.

Conversely the != inequality operator returns 1 (true) if two operands are not equal, using the same rules as the == equality operator, otherwise it returns 0 (false).

Equality and inequality operators are useful in testing the state of two variables to perform conditional branching in a program.

The > "greater than" operator compares two operands and will return 1 (true) if the first is greater in value than the second, or it will return 0 (false) if it is equal or less in value. The > "greater than" operator is frequently used to test the value of a countdown value in a loop.

The < "less than" operators makes the same comparison but returns 1 (true) if the first operand is less in value than the second, otherwise it returns 0 (false).

Adding the = operator after a > "greater than" or < "less than" operator makes it also return true if the two operands are exactly equal in value.

This example demonstrates each comparison operator in action:

```c
#include <stdio.h>
int main()
{

    int a = 0, b = 0, c = 1; char d = 'A', e = 'a';

printf("Equality example:\n");
printf("\tIs a equal to b? (0==0) %d (true) \n",a==b);
printf("\tIs d equal to e? (A==a) %d (false)\n",d==e);
printf("Inequality example:\n\tIs a not equal to c?");
printf("(0!=1) %d (true)\n", a != c );
printf("Greater than example:\nIs a greater than c?");
printf("(0>1) %d (false) \n", a > c );
printf("Less than example:\n\tIs a less than c? ");
printf("(0<1) %d (true) \n", a < c );
printf("Greater than or equal to example:\n");
printf("\tIs a greater than or equal to b? ");
printf(" (0>=0) %d (true) \n", a >= b );
printf("Less than or equal to example:\n");
printf("\tIs c less than or equal to a? ");
printf("(1<=0) %d (false) \n", c <= a );

    return 0;
}
```

comparison.c

49

```
Command Prompt                                    - □ ×
C:\MyPrograms>gcc comparison.c -o comparison.exe

C:\MyPrograms>comparison
Equality example:
        Is a equal to b? (0==0) 1 (true)
        Is d equal to e? (A==a) 0 (false)
Inequality example:
        Is a not equal to c? (0!=1) 1 (true)
Greater than example:
        Is a greater than c? (0>1) 0 (false)
Less than example:
        Is a less than c? (0<1) 1 (true)
Greater than or equal to example:
        Is a greater than or equal to b?  (0>=0) 1
Less than or equal to example:
        Is c less than or equal to a? (1<=0) 0 (fa

C:\MyPrograms>_
```

Conditional operator

Possibly the C programmer's favorite test operator is the ?: "conditional" operator. This operator first evaluates an expression for a true or false value then executes one of two given statements depending on the result of the evaluation.

The conditional operator has this syntax:

(*test-expression*) ? *if-true-do-this* : *if-false-do-this* ;

This operator is used to execute program statements according to the result of its conditional test. The example below evaluates two integer variable values to determine if they are odd or even numbers. The program outputs an appropriate message according to the result of the test.

```c
#include <stdio.h>
int main()
{
    int num1 = 13579, num2 = 24680;
    char letter;

    ( num1 %2 != 0 ) ? printf("%d is odd\n",num1) :
                        printf("%d is even\n",num2);

    ( num2 %2 != 0 ) ? printf("%d is odd\n",num2) :
                        printf("%d is even\n",num2);

    letter = ( num2 %2 != 0 ) ? 'Y' : 'N';
    printf("Is %d odd?: %c\n", num2, letter);

    return 0;
}
```

conditional.c

Hot tip

In this example the first two instances of the conditional operator execute the relevant printf() function call, whereas the final conditional test assigns the appropriate character value to the letter variable.

```
Command Prompt                                    _ □ ✕

C:\MyPrograms>gcc conditional.c -o conditional.exe

C:\MyPrograms>conditional
13579 is odd
24680 is even
Is 24680 odd?: N

C:\MyPrograms>_
```

The sizeof operator

The sizeof operator returns an integer value that is the number of bytes needed to store the contents of its operand. The operand can be a data type contained inside parentheses, as in the earlier example on page 25, or an expression without parentheses, as seen in the following example. The sizeof operator is used here to ascertain the size, in bytes, of various objects in the program:

```c
#include <stdio.h>

struct person {char name[50]; int age; float height;};

int main()
{
  int num = 1234567890;
  float dec = 0.123456;
  double ext = 0.0123456789;
  char ltr = 'A';
  char str[] = "Something to write home about...";
  struct person boy;

printf("Size of num int is %d bytes\n",    sizeof num);
printf("Size of dec float is %d bytes\n", sizeof dec);
printf("Size of ext double is %d bytes\n",sizeof ext);
printf("Size of ltr char is %d byte\n",    sizeof ltr);
printf("Size of str string is %d bytes\n",sizeof str);
printf("Size of boy struct is %d bytes\n",sizeof boy);

  return 0;
}
```

sizeofop.c

Hot tip

This example includes code for a struct object, which is a list of different data type variables. Structs are demonstrated in chapter 10 but the struct object is included here to demonstrate that the sizeof operator can ascertain the size of a struct object.

```
Command Prompt                                    _ □ ✕
C:\MyPrograms>gcc sizeofop.c -o sizeofop.exe

C:\MyPrograms>sizeofop
Size of num int is 4 bytes
Size of dec float is 4 bytes
Size of ext double is 8 bytes
Size of ltr char is 1 byte
Size of str string is 33 bytes
Size of boy struct is 60 bytes

C:\MyPrograms>_
```

Operator precedence

Operator precedence defines the order in which C evaluates expressions. For instance, in the expression a=6+b*3, the order of precedence determines whether the addition or the multiplication is completed first. The table below gives the precedence in decreasing order – operators on the top row have the highest precedence, those on lower rows have successively lower precedence. Operators on the same row have equal precedence.

Operator	Associativity
( ) function call [ ] array index -> struct pointer . struct member	Left to right
! NOT ~ bitwise NOT ++ increment – – decrement + positive sign **sizeof** – negative sign * pointer & addressof	Right to left
* multiply / divide % modulus	Left to right
+ add – subtract	Left to right
<< left shift >> right shift	Left to right
< less than <= less or equal > greater than >= greater or equal	Left to right
== equality != inequality	Left to right
& bitwise AND	Left to right
^ bitwise XOR	Left to right
| bitwise OR	Left to right
&& AND	Left to right
|| OR	Left to right
?: conditional	Right to left
= += –= *= /= %= &= ^= |= <<= >>= all assignment operators	Right to left
, comma	Left to right

Hot tip

The * multiply operator is on a higher row than the + add operator – so in the expression a=6+b*3 the multiplication is carried out before the addition.

Hot tip

The struct operators and bitwise operators appear later in this book but are included here to provide a complete precedence table of all operators.

Making statements

This chapter introduces the "statement" and demonstrates how a C program can evaluate an expression to determine the direction in which the program should proceed.

Conditional if statement

The if keyword is used to perform the basic conditional test that evaluates a given expression for a boolean value of true or false. Statements following the evaluation will only be executed when the expression is found to be true.

The syntax for the if statement looks like this:

if (*test-expression*) { *code-to-be-executed-when-true* }

The code to be executed may be multiple statements, all contained within the braces, each ending with a semi-colon.

In the example program below the test expression evaluates whether one number is greater than another.

If the first number is, in fact, greater than the second number the expression will be true so the statements inside the braces following the test will be executed.

If the expression was false the statements following the test would not be executed and the program would just move on to the next test, or statement, in the code.

Hot tip

When the code to be executed is just a single statement the braces may, optionally, be omitted.

iftest.c

```c
#include <stdio.h>

int main()
{
  if ( 5 > 1 )
  {
    printf("Yes, 5 is greater than 1\n");
    printf("Thanks for asking!\n");
  }

  return 0;
}
```

Hot tip

The test expression in this example could alternatively be if(1<5) – testing, is 1 less than 5.

```
Command Prompt                                    _ □ ✕
C:\MyPrograms>gcc iftest.c -o iftest.exe

C:\MyPrograms>iftest
Yes, 5 is greater than 1
Thanks for asking!

C:\MyPrograms>_
```

Nesting if statements

Conditional if statements can be nested inside other if statement blocks to test multiple expressions. In this example the three statements calling the printf() function will only be executed when all three tested expressions are true.

```c
#include <stdio.h>

int main()
{
  if ( 5 > 1 )
  {
      if( 'A' == 'A' )
      {
          if( 1 != 0 )
          {
            printf("Yes, 5 is greater than 1 \n");
            printf("and A is equal to A \n");
            printf("and 1 does not equal 0 \n");
          }
      }
  }
  return 0;
}
```

ifnest.c

Beware

Be sure to use the == equality operator to test for equality, rather than the = assignment operator.

55

```
Command Prompt                          _ □ ×
C:\MyPrograms>gcc ifnest.c -o ifnest.exe

C:\MyPrograms>ifnest
Yes, 5 is greater than 1
and A is equal to A
and 1 does not equal 0

C:\MyPrograms>_
```

An alternative method to evaluate multiple expressions with an if statement employs the && logical AND operator. The evaluations in the program above could be made in a single test like this:

```c
if( ( 5 > 1 ) && ( 'A'=='A' ) && ( 1 != 0 ) ) { ... }
```

Don't forget

When testing multiple expressions enclose each expression inside parentheses.

If-else statement

The else keyword can be used with an if statement to specify alternative code to be executed in the event that the test expression is false. This is known as "conditional branching" because the program will branch along a certain route according to a test condition. The syntax of an if-else statement looks like this:

if (*test-expression*) { *do-this-if-true* } else { *do-this-if-false* }

Several expressions can be tested using successive else if statements until a true value is found – whereon the statements following that test will be executed. The following example demonstrates how the if-else statement ends after one test is found to be true and its statements have been executed:

ifelse.c

```c
#include <stdio.h>
int main()
{
  int num = 2, bool = 0;
  if ( (num == 2) && (bool) )
  {
    printf("The first test is untrue\n");
  }
  else if( (num == 2) && (!bool) )
  {
    printf("The second test is true\n");
  }
  else if( (num == 2) && (bool == 0) )
  {
    printf("The third test is true but unreached\n");
  }
  return 0;
}
```

Hot tip

This example uses shorthand for boolean values – (bool) is true shorthand for (bool == 1) and (!bool) is false shorthand for (bool==0).

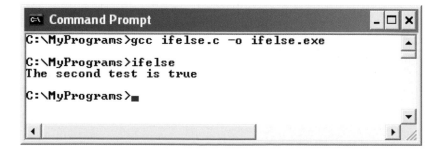

```
C:\MyPrograms>gcc ifelse.c -o ifelse.exe

C:\MyPrograms>ifelse
The second test is true

C:\MyPrograms>_
```

Switch statement

Conditional branching with long if-else statements can often be more efficiently performed using a switch statement instead when the test expression just evaluates a single integer.

The switch statement works in an unusual way. It takes a given integer value then seeks a matching value among a number of case statements.

Code associated with the matching case statement will be executed or default code may execute if no match is found.

Each case statement must end with a break statement to prevent the program continuing through the switch block.

This program gets a single character value from the user then executes the appropriate case statement code:

```c
#include <stdio.h>
int main()
{
  char letter;
  printf("Enter any single character: ");
  scanf("%c", &letter);

  switch(letter)
  {
    case 'a' : printf("Letter \'a\' found\n"); break;
    case 'b' : printf("Letter \'b\' found\n"); break;
    case 'c' : printf("Letter \'c\' found\n"); break;
    default  : printf("The letter is not a,b or c\n");
  }
  return 0;
}
```

```
Command Prompt                              _ □ ✕
C:\MyPrograms>gcc switch.c -o switch.exe

C:\MyPrograms>switch
Enter any single character: b
Letter 'b' found

C:\MyPrograms>
```

Don't forget

Each character is represented by the integer value of its ASCII code number – see page 162.

switch.c

Beware

Quotes nested within other quotes must be escaped with the backslash character to avoid confusing the compiler.

The for loop

A loop is a piece of code in a program that automatically repeats. One complete execution of all the statements within a loop is called an "iteration", or a "pass".

The length of a loop is controlled by a conditional test made within the loop. While the tested expression is true the loop will continue – until the test expression is found to be false when the loop ends.

In C there are three types of loops – for loops, while loops and do-while loops. Perhaps the most common of these is the for loop, which typically has this syntax:

for (*initializer* ; *test-expression* ; *increment*) { *statements* }

The initializer is used to set a starting value for a counter of the number of iterations made by the loop. An integer variable is used for this purpose and is traditionally named "i".

Upon each iteration of the loop the test-expression is evaluated and that iteration will only continue while this expression is true. When the test-expression becomes false the loop ends immediately without executing the statements again. With every iteration the counter is incremented then the loop's statements are executed.

The example below demonstrates a for loop that outputs the number of the current iteration on each pass. When the counter reaches 3 the test-expression becomes false so the loop is terminated. The output is shown on the next page together with a further example demonstrating how for loops can be nested.

Hot tip

Alternatively, a for loop counter can count downwards by decrementing the counter value on each pass using i-- instead of i++.

58

forloop.c

```c
#include <stdio.h>

int main()
{
    int i;

    for( i = 0; i < 3; i++ )
    {
        printf("For loop iteration number %d\n", i );
    }
    return 0;
}
```

```
Command Prompt                                    _ □ ✕
C:\MyPrograms>gcc forloop.c -o forloop.exe        ▲

C:\MyPrograms>forloop
For loop iteration number 0
For loop iteration number 1
For loop iteration number 2

C:\MyPrograms>_                                   ▼
◄                                              ►
```

```c
#include <stdio.h>
int main()
{
  int i,j;

  for( i = 1; i < 4; i++ )
  {
    printf("Outer loop iteration number %d\n", i);

    for( j = 1; j < 4; j++ )
    {
      printf("\tInner loop iteration number %d\n", j);
    }

  }
  return 0;
}
```

fornest.c

```
Command Prompt                                    _ □ ✕
C:\MyPrograms>gcc fornest.c -o fornest.exe        ▲

C:\MyPrograms>fornest
Outer loop iteration number 1
        Inner loop iteration number 1
        Inner loop iteration number 2
        Inner loop iteration number 3
Outer loop iteration number 2
        Inner loop iteration number 1
        Inner loop iteration number 2
        Inner loop iteration number 3
Outer loop iteration number 3
        Inner loop iteration number 1
        Inner loop iteration number 2
        Inner loop iteration number 3

C:\MyPrograms>_                                   ▼
◄                                              ►
```

While loop

Another type of loop uses the while keyword followed by an expression to be evaluated for a true or false value.

If the expression is found to be true then the statements contained within braces following the tested expression will be executed. After the statements have all been executed the test-expression will again be evaluated and the loop will continue until the test-expression is found to be false.

The loop's statement block must contain code that will affect the test-expression in order to change the evaluation result to false, otherwise an infinite loop is created which will lock the system.

Note that if the test expression is found to be false when it is first evaluated the code in the statement block is never executed.

The example below decrements two variable values on each iteration and decrements the counter until it reaches zero – whereon the evaluation is found to be false so the loop ends.

Don't forget

Changing the
i-- decrementer to an
i++ incrementer in
this example will create
an infinite loop. In this
case, on either Windows
or Linux systems, press
Ctrl+C keyboard keys to
halt the program.

while.c

```c
#include <stdio.h>

int main()
{
   int a = 30, b = 15, i = 3;

   while ( i > 0 )
   {
      a -= 10; b -=5; i--;
      printf("Variable a is %d variable b is %d\n",a,b);
   }
   return 0;
}
```

```
Command Prompt
C:\MyPrograms>gcc while.c -o while.exe

C:\MyPrograms>while
Variable a is 20 variable b is 10
Variable a is 10 variable b is 5
Variable a is 0 variable b is 0

C:\MyPrograms>
```

Do-while loop

The do-while loop is a subtle variation of the while loop described on the opposite page. In this loop the do keyword is followed by a statement block within braces containing all the statements to be executed on each iteration.

The statement block is then followed by the while keyword and an expression to be evaluated for a true or false value. If the expression is found to be true the loop continues from the do keyword until the test-expression is found to be false – whereon the loop ends.

Note that, unlike the while loop, the statements in the do-while loop's statement block will always be executed at least once because the test-expression is not found until the end of the loop.

The following example will never loop because the counter value is incremented to 1 in the very first execution of the statement block – so the test-expression is found to be false at the first test.

```c
#include <stdio.h>

int main()
{
  int a = 0, i = 0;

  do
  {
    ++a;
    ++i;
    printf("Variable a is %d", a);
  }
  while ( i < 1 );

  return 0;
}
```

dowhile.c

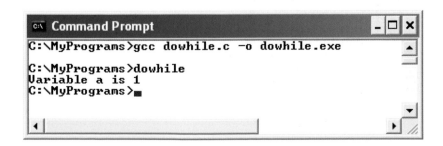

```
C:\MyPrograms>gcc dowhile.c -o dowhile.exe

C:\MyPrograms>dowhile
Variable a is 1
C:\MyPrograms>_
```

Hot tip

A while loop is often more suitable than a do-while loop because its statements are not automatically executed on the first iteration.

Break statement

The break keyword was introduced on page 57 to exit individual case statements inside a switch statement block. It has a further important use, however, to exit from any loop.

A break statement can be included inside any loop statement block, preceded by a conditional test. When that test is found to be true the break statement immediately terminates the loop and no further iterations will be made.

In the following example a while loop is set to complete 10 iterations, but when the counter reaches 7 the break statement terminates the loop at once.

dobreak.c

Don't forget

A break statement stops a loop instantly – no further iterations are made.

```c
#include <stdio.h>

int main()
{
  int i = 0;

  while ( i < 10 )
  {
    ++i;
    printf("Loop iteration is %d",i);

    /* if the counter hits 7 end this loop now */
    if( i == 7 ) break;

    printf("Go to the next pass\n");
  }
  return 0;
}
```

```
Command Prompt                                    _ □ ✕
C:\MyPrograms>gcc dobreak.c -o dobreak.exe

C:\MyPrograms>dobreak
Loop iteration is 1 - go to the next pass
Loop iteration is 2 - go to the next pass
Loop iteration is 3 - go to the next pass
Loop iteration is 4 - go to the next pass
Loop iteration is 5 - go to the next pass
Loop iteration is 6 - go to the next pass
Loop iteration is 7
C:\MyPrograms>_
```

Continue statement

The C language continue keyword can be used to interrupt the execution of a loop but has one important difference to the break keyword described opposite – the continue keyword only stops the execution of the current iteration of a loop.

Just like in a break statement, the continue keyword is preceded by a conditional test within the loop's statement block. When its test-expression is found to be true the current iteration is terminated immediately and the next iteration then begins.

Note that the loop counter must be changed before a continue test-expression is encountered to avoid creating an infinite loop.

In the following example the test-expression is found to be true when the counter value reaches 3 – so that iteration of the loop is skipped but the loop continues to complete its other passes.

```c
#include <stdio.h>

int main()
{
    int i = 0;

    while ( i < 6 )
    {
        ++i;
        if ( i == 3 ) continue;
        printf("Loop iteration is %d",i);
        printf(" - go to the next pass\n");
    }
    return 0;
}
```

continue.c

```
Command Prompt

C:\MyPrograms>gcc continue.c -o continue.exe

C:\MyPrograms>continue
Loop iteration is 1 - go to the next pass
Loop iteration is 2 - go to the next pass
Loop iteration is 4 - go to the next pass
Loop iteration is 5 - go to the next pass
Loop iteration is 6 - go to the next pass

C:\MyPrograms>
```

The infamous goto label

The goto keyword supposedly allows the program flow to jump to labels at other points in the program, much like a hyperlink on a web page. However, in reality this can cause errors, its use is much-frowned upon and considered bad programming practice.

One possible valid use of the goto keyword is to break cleanly from a nested loop. This is demonstrated in the example below which instantly exits both nested loops in the example listed on page 59.

On the whole, though, it should not be used and no other example in this book features the hapless goto keyword.

dogoto.c

Hot tip

The goto keyword has existed in computer programs for decades. Its power was abused by many early programmers who created programs that jumped around in an unfathomable manner. This created unreadable programs so the use of goto became hugely unpopular, and this remains so today.

```c
#include <stdio.h>

int main()
{
  int i, j;

  for( i = 1; i < 4; i++ )
  {
    printf("Outer loop iteration number %d\n", i);
    for( j = 1; j < 4; j++ )
    {
      if( j == 3 ) goto end;    /* jump to label */
      printf("\tInner loop iteration number %d\n", j);
    }
  }

  /* label */
  end:

  return 0;
}
```

```
C:\MyPrograms>gcc dogoto.c -o dogoto.exe

C:\MyPrograms>dogoto
Outer loop iteration number 1
        Inner loop iteration number 1
        Inner loop iteration number 2

C:\MyPrograms>
```

6 Using functions

This chapter introduces the "function" and demonstrates how statements contained within a function are executed whenever that function is called upon by the C program.

Function declaration

Previous examples in this book have used the obligatory main() function and standard functions contained in the C header library, such as the printf() function from the stdio.h file. However, most C programs contain a number of custom functions which can be called as required during the execution of the program.

Functions simply contain a group of statements which are executed whenever the function is called. Once their statements have been executed program flow resumes at the point the function was called. This modularity is very useful in programming to separate set routines so they can be used repeatedly.

To introduce a custom function into a program it must first be declared, in a similar manner that variables must be declared before they can be used. Function declarations should be added to the program code before the main() function.

Like the main() function, custom functions can return a value. The data type of this value must be included in the function declaration. If the function is to return no value its return data type should be declared with the void keyword. The function should be named following the same naming conventions used for variable names.

The function declaration is more correctly called the "function prototype" and simply informs the compiler about the function. The actual function definition, which includes the statements to be executed, appears after the main() function. The custom function can then be called upon to execute its statements from within the main() function, as required.

If a custom function returns a value this can be assigned to a variable of the appropriate data type, or simply displayed as output using the appropriate format specifier.

The following example declares three custom functions called first(), square5() and cube5().

The first() function just outputs a message when called but returns no value. The square5() function returns an integer value that is assigned to an int variable, whose value is subsequently displayed as output by the printf() function. The cube5() function also returns an integer value which is directly output by printf().

Hot tip

The function prototype is also sometimes referred to as the "function header".

```c
#include <stdio.h>

void first();          /* declare function prototypes */
int square5();
int cube5();

int main()                      /* define main function */
{
  int num;
  first();                          /* call function */
  num = square5();                  /* call function */
  printf("5x5= %d\n",num);
  printf("5x5x5= %d\n",cube5() ); /* call function */
  return 0;
}

void first()              /* define custom function */
{
  printf("Hello from my first() function\n");
}

int square5()             /* define custom function */
{
  int square = 5*5;
  return square;
}

int cube5()               /* define custom function */
{
  int cube = (5*5)*5;
  return cube;
}
```

first.c

Don't forget

Notice that each function prototype must end with a semi-colon.

67

Hot tip

The custom function definitions could technically appear before the main() function without prototypes – but the convention is to include prototypes and keep the main() function at the beginning of the program.

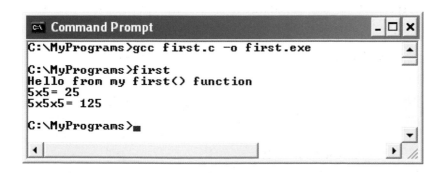

```
Command Prompt                                    _ □ ×
C:\MyPrograms>gcc first.c -o first.exe

C:\MyPrograms>first
Hello from my first() function
5x5= 25
5x5x5= 125

C:\MyPrograms>
```

Function arguments

Data can be passed as arguments to custom functions who can then use that data to execute their statements. The function prototype must include the name and data type of each argument.

It is important to recognize that in C programming the data is passed "by value" to the variable specified as the function argument. This is different to some other programming languages, such as Pascal, whose arguments are passed "by reference" – where the function has access to the original data, not just a local copy.

The arguments in a function prototype are known as the "formal parameters" of the function. These may be of different data types and multiple arguments can be specified for a single function if separated by a comma. For example, a function prototype with arguments of each of the four data types could look like this:

```
void action( char c, int i, float f, double d );
```

The compiler checks that the formal parameters specified in the function's prototype match those of the actual function definition and will report an error if they do not match.

The example listed on the opposite page creates three custom functions with one argument each.

The display() function has an argument named str that is an array of the char data type, capable of storing a string of text. Inside the main() function a string is assigned to another array named msg. When the display() function is called, the string in the msg variable is passed to the str variable, which is then displayed by a call to the printf() function.

Both other custom functions, square() and cube(), have a single argument of the int data type. When these functions are called from within the main() function an integer value is passed to their argument. This value is used in a piece of arithmetic then the result is returned to the main() function. The call to the square() function assigns the returned value to an int variable – which is subsequently displayed by the printf() function. The call to the cube() function is itself made from within a call to the printf() function so is immediately displayed.

```c
#include <stdio.h>

void display(char str[]);     /* function prototypes */
int square(int x);
int cube(int y);

int main()                    /* define main function */
{
  char msg[50]=
            "This string gets passed to a function";
  int num;

  display(msg);                     /* call function */
  num = square(4);                  /* call function */
  printf("4x4= %d\n", num);
  printf("4x4x4= %d\n", cube(4) ); /* call function */
  return 0;
}

void display(char str[]) /* define custom function */
{
  printf("%s\n", str);
}

int square(int x)        /* define custom function */
{
  return (x*x);
}

int cube(int y)          /* define custom function */
{
  return (y*y)*y;
}
```

args.c

69

Hot tip

A function need not return any value but can include the return keyword without any following expression to signify the return of control.

Calling other functions

Custom functions can freely call other custom functions, just as readily as they can call standard library functions like printf().

This is demonstrated in the example below that calls a custom function named getnum() from within the main() function. That function in turn calls another custom function named square() during the execution of its statements.

multi.c

```c
#include <stdio.h>

void getnum();                      /* function prototypes */
int square(int x);

int main()                          /* define main function */
{
    getnum();                       /* call function */
    printf("End\n");
    return 0;
}

void getnum()                   /* define custom function */
{
    int num;
    printf("Enter an integer to be squared: ");
    scanf("%d", &num);
    printf("%d squared is %d\n", num, square(num) );
}

int square(int x)           /* define custom function */
{
    return (x*x);
}
```

Hot tip

This example finishes by printing "End" to illustrate that control finally returns to the main() function.

```
Command Prompt                                    _ □ ✕
C:\MyPrograms>gcc multi.c -o multi.exe

C:\MyPrograms>multi
Enter an integer to be squared: 5
5 squared is 25
End

C:\MyPrograms>■
```

Recursive functions

Functions that call themselves are known as "recursive" functions. As with a loop the function must modify a tested condition to avoid locking the program.

A recursive function is included in the example program listed below. It outputs the current value of a positive integer variable from a starting point entered by the user. That value is decremented with each call of the function until it reaches -1, at which point control is returned to the main() function.

```c
#include <stdio.h>

void count_down_from(int x); /* function prototypes */

int main()                   /* define main function */
{
 int num;
 printf("Enter a positive integer
                      to count down from:");
 scanf("%d", &num);
 count_down_from(num);            /* call function */
 return 0;
}

void count_down_from(int x)      /* define function */
{
 printf("%d\n", x);
 --x;
 if( x < 0 ) return;
 else count_down_from(x);     /* call recursively */
}
```

recur.c

Hot tip

A recursive function can be less efficient than using a loop.

```
Command Prompt                              _ □ ✕

C:\MyPrograms>gcc recur.c -o recur.exe

C:\MyPrograms>recur
Enter a positive integer to count down from: 4
4
3
2
1
0

C:\MyPrograms>_
```

Functions in custom headers

The example programs illustrated throughout this book are necessarily small due to space considerations but in reality most C programs will contain significantly more code.

When developing larger programs some thought should be given to program structure. Maintaining the entire program code in a single file can become unwieldy as the program grows.

In order to simplify the program structure a custom header file can be created to contain functions which may be used repeatedly. This should be named with a ".h" file extension, like the standard header files in the C library.

The functions in the custom header file can be made available to the main program file by adding an #include preprocessor directive at the beginning of that file. The custom header file name should be enclosed within double quotes though, rather than the < and > angled brackets used to include standard header files.

To illustrate a custom header the program listed on the opposite page builds on the one listed on page 70. The square() function has now been removed from the main program and placed in a custom header file named utils.h, shown below:

utils.h

```
/* This header file contains utility functions */

int square( int x );          /* function prototype */

int square( int x )           /* function definition */
{
  return (x*x);
}
```

The custom header file function is made available to the program with the #include "utils.h" preprocessor directive at the beginning of the program. In this version of the program the user is given the opportunity to complete multiple calculations of square values. Each one is completed by a call to the square() function inside the custom header file.

The code within the main() function itself is kept to a minimum which indicates an efficient program structure.

```c
#include <stdio.h>
#include "utils.h"

void getnum();

int main()
{
   getnum();
   printf("End\n");
   return 0;
}

void getnum()
{
   int num;
   char again;
   const char OK = 'Y', ok = 'y';

   printf("Enter an integer to be squared: ");
   scanf("%d", &num);
   printf("%d squared is %d\n", num, square(num) );

   printf("Square another number?, Y or N:");
   scanf("%1s", &again);

   if( ( again == OK ) || ( again == ok ) ) getnum();
   else return;
}
```

square.c

Hot tip

Notice the use of the %1s format specifier in this example – this reads the next character entered by the user.

73

```
Command Prompt                              _ □ ×
C:\MyPrograms>gcc square.c -o square.exe

C:\MyPrograms>square
Enter an integer to be squared: 7
7 squared is 49
Square another number?, Y or N:y
Enter an integer to be squared: 8
8 squared is 64
Square another number?, Y or N:y
Enter an integer to be squared: 9
9 squared is 81
Square another number?, Y or N:n
End

C:\MyPrograms>_
```

Multiple source files

Programs may comprise multiple source code files to make them more manageable. The following program source code files build on the previous example to allow the user to select an operation from a menu.

The main file calls a function named menu() that is in a file named menu.c. When the user selects an operation its respective function is called from another file named ops.c. The functions that actually perform the arithmetic are located in the utils.h custom header file.

Compilation of multiple source code files is slightly different to that used for single files. The technique to compile these programs into a single executable file is demonstrated on page 76.

calc.c

```c
#include <stdio.h>

int main()
{
    menu();
    printf("End\n");
    return 0;
}
```

menu.c

```c
#include <stdio.h>

void menu();

void menu()
{
    int num;
    printf("\n\tEnter the number of an operation:\n");
    printf("\t1. Square a number\n");
    printf("\t2. Multiply two numbers\n");
    printf("\t3. Exit\n");
    scanf("%d",&num);

    switch(num)
    {
        case 1 : getnum(); break;
        case 2 : getnums(); break;
        case 3 : return;
    }
}
```

Hot tip

If the user selects option 3 control returns to the main() function and the program ends.

```c
#include <stdio.h>
#include "utils.h"

void getnum();
void getnums();

void getnum()
{
  int num;
  printf("Enter an integer to be squared: ");
  scanf("%d", &num);
  printf("%d squared is %d\n", num, square(num) );
  menu();
}

void getnums()
{
  int num1, num2;
  printf("Enter 2 numbers to be multiplied, ");
  printf("separated by a space: ");
  scanf("%d", &num1);
  scanf("%d", &num2);
  printf("%dx%d= %d\n",num1,num2,multiply(num1,num2));
  menu();
}
```

```c
/* This header file contains utility functions */

int square(int x);          /* function prototypes */
int multiply(int x, int y);

int square(int x)           /* function definitions */
{
  return (x*x);
}

int multiply(int x, int y)
{
  return (x*y);
}
```

An illustration of this program in action appears on page 77.

ops.c

Hot tip

If the user selects menu option 1 or 2 the appropriate function code is executed. Finally the menu() function is called once more to again display the options.

75

utils.h

Don't forget

The header file does not need to be compiled itself – its functionality is incorporated into the program by the compiler.

Linking files

Although compilers do vary in the way they operate, the process of creating an executable file from source code involves these three basic stages:

- First the preprocessor is called upon to execute all the preprocessor directives. These includes header files, execute macros and carry out any definition substitutions

- Next the compiler creates a compiled temporary file for each source code file. These are known as object files and normally have the file extension of ".o" or ".obj"

- After creating all the object files the process calls upon an application called a "linker". This is included with each compiler and links together all the object files to create the final single executable program file.

The process can be controlled manually using a -c switch in the command given to the compiler. This switch tells the compiler to create an object file, but not to call the linker application. For instance, the command gcc -c test.c -o test.o creates a compiled object file named test.o from a source code file named test.c.

For programs that have multiple source code files, such as the example on the previous page, individual commands can be issued to create the object files one by one, like this:

> gcc -c calc.c -o calc.o

> gcc -c menu.c -o menu.o

> gcc -c ops.c -o ops.o

Now that the object files are all in place they can be linked together to create the executable program file with the single command gcc calc.o menu.o ops.o -o calc.exe

This will then build the file calc.exe which can be executed as normal, using the commands calc or calc.exe, on Windows, and the command ./calc.exe on Linux.

The illustration on the opposite page shows the compilation process and demonstrates the program in action.

Don't forget

The -c switch means "compile only" and the -o switch means "output as".

calc.o menu.o ops.o

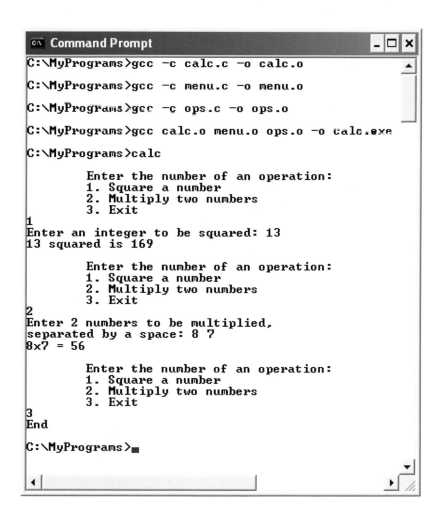

```
Command Prompt                              _ □ ×

C:\MyPrograms>gcc -c calc.c -o calc.o

C:\MyPrograms>gcc -c menu.c -o menu.o

C:\MyPrograms>gcc -c ops.c -o ops.o

C:\MyPrograms>gcc calc.o menu.o ops.o -o calc.exe

C:\MyPrograms>calc

        Enter the number of an operation:
        1. Square a number
        2. Multiply two numbers
        3. Exit
1
Enter an integer to be squared: 13
13 squared is 169

        Enter the number of an operation:
        1. Square a number
        2. Multiply two numbers
        3. Exit
2
Enter 2 numbers to be multiplied,
separated by a space: 8 7
8x7 = 56

        Enter the number of an operation:
        1. Square a number
        2. Multiply two numbers
        3. Exit
3
End

C:\MyPrograms>_
```

Hot tip

It is a simple matter to enlarge this program because its components are in separate files – add extra menu items to menu.c, add extra operations to ops.c, add arithmetic functions to the utils.h header file.

77

It is worthwhile understanding how the compilation process creates object files that are then linked to create the final executable file.

Typing all these commands is, however, somewhat tedious –especially in large programs that have lots of source code files.

Fortunately, the whole process can be achieved with one single command. For instance, to create the calc.exe file in the example illustrated above, type this single command:

gcc calc.c menu.c ops.c -o calc.exe

Hot tip

The GNU C compiler destroys the object files after the executable is created using this method. Other C compilers, such as the Microsoft C compiler may not destroy the object files.

Static functions

The static keyword can be used to restrict the accessibility of functions to the file in which they are created, in exactly the same way that static variables have restricted accessibility.

To demonstrate this the example below declares and defines a static function called secret() in the second.c file. This can be called by the call_external() function located in the same file. Attempting to call the secret() function from within the main.c file is not permitted and the compiler would not compile that program.

Hot tip

For more information on static variables please refer to page 27.

main.c

```c
#include <stdio.h>

int main()
{
  printf("Hello from the main file\n");
  call_external();
  return 0;
}
```

second.c

```c
#include <stdio.h>

static int secret();

void call_external()
{
  printf("Secret number is %d\n", secret() );
}

static int secret()
{
  return 12345;
}
```

```
C:\ Command Prompt                                    _ □ ✗

C:\MyPrograms>gcc main.c second.c -o statfun.exe

C:\MyPrograms>statfun
Hello from the main file
Secret number is 12345

C:\MyPrograms>█
```

7 Working with bits

This chapter introduces the "bitwise" operators and demonstrates how they can be used in C programs to perform binary arithmetic.

Decimal & hexadecimal

The decimal system

The decimal numbering system, that we use everyday, has a "base" of ten comprising the digits 0 to 9. This probably evolved because we have ten fingers – so it's logical and comfortable to base a numbering system around the value of ten.

For instance, with the number 8,452 we see "eight thousand four hundred and fifty two". This can be expressed as "eight lots of thousands", "four lots of hundreds", "five lots of tens", and "two lots of units", or arithmetically:

```
(8 x 1000) + (4 x 100) + (5 x 10) + (2 x 1) = 8,452
```

Alternatively, this number can be expressed by representing the units, tens, hundreds and thousands as powers of 10, like this:

$$(8 \times 10^3) + (4 \times 10^2) + (5 \times 10^1) + (2 \times 10^0) = 8,452$$

Notice how the power value increments from right to left.

The hexadecimal system

Unlike the decimal system, hexadecimal has a base number of 16. This system still uses the digits 0 to 9 but also uses the letters A, B, C, D, E and F to represent the decimal numbers 10, 11, 12, 13, 14 and 15 respectively.

For instance, hexadecimal B is the same value as decimal 11.

It is common to clarify the intended numbering system by suffixing the system's base number in subscript – so that 24_{10} indicates the decimal system is being used, whereas 24_{16} indicates the hexadecimal system is being used. With 24_{10} there are two lots of tens and four lots of units, like this:

```
( 2 x 10 ) + ( 4 x 1 ) = 24
```

With 24_{16} there are two lots of sixteen and four lots of units:

```
( 2 x 16 ) + ( 4 x 1 ) = 36 in decimal
```

So 24 in the hexadecimal system is equivalent to decimal 36 and could be expressed like this:

$$(2 \times 16^1) + (4 \times 16^0) = 36$$

Hot tip

Uppercase is commonly used for hexadecimal A, B, C, D, E and F because it appears more readable – lowercase a, b, c, d, e and f would also be valid though.

The conversion of hexadecimal numbers to decimal requires knowledge of the decimal value of powers of 16, listed below:

Powers of 16	Hexadecimal	Decimal value
16^0	1	1
16^1	10	16
16^2	100	256
16^3	1000	4096
16^4	10000	65536

Hot tip

Also octal numbers have a base value of 8 and can be displayed with the %o format specifier.

For instance, the hexadecimal value $112F_{16}$ can be converted as:

```
1 = ( 1 x 16³ ), or ( 1 x 4096 )      4096
1 = ( 1 x 16² ), or ( 1 x 256 )        256
2 = ( 2 x 16¹ ), or ( 2 x 16 )          32
F = ( 15 x 16⁰ ), or ( 15 x 1 )         15
112F hexadecimal =                    4399 decimal
```

In C programming, hexadecimal numbers are indicated with the prefix "0x" and can be displayed using the format specifier of %x, for lowercase representation, or %X for uppercase representation.

```c
#include <stdio.h>

int main()
{
   printf("%d is %X in hexadecimal", 0x112F, 0x112F);
   return 0;
}
```

hex.c

Binary numbering

The binary numbering system is the basic numbering system used by computers and has a base of 2. This means that all numbers are represented by just zeros and ones.

Counting up, decimal 1 = binary 1, decimal 2 = binary 10, decimal 3 = binary 11, decimal 4 = binary 100, decimal 5 = binary 101, decimal 6 = binary 110, decimal 7 = binary 111, etc..

The conversion of binary numbers to decimal requires knowledge of the decimal value of powers of 2, listed in this table:

Hot tip

To a computer a zero is an "off" state and a one is an "on" state.

Powers of 2	Binary	Decimal value
2^0	1	1
2^1	10	2
2^2	100	4
2^3	1000	8
2^4	10000	16
2^5	100000	32
2^6	1000000	64
2^7	10000000	128
2^8	100000000	258
2^9	1000000000	512
2^{10}	10000000000	1024
2^{11}	100000000000	2048
2^{12}	1000000000000	4096
2^{13}	10000000000000	8192
2^{14}	100000000000000	16384
2^{15}	1000000000000000	32768
2^{16}	10000000000000000	65536

For instance, the binary value 10110_2 can be converted as:

```
1 = ( 1 x 2⁴ ), or ( 1 x 16 )        16
0 = ( 0 x 2³ ), or ( 0 x 8 )          0
1 = ( 1 x 2² ), or ( 1 x 4 )          4
1 = ( 1 x 2¹ ), or ( 1 x 2 )          2
0 = ( 0 x 2⁰ ), or ( 0 x 1 )          0
10110 binary =                       22 decimal
```

Converting decimal to binary, find the highest power of 2 that will go into a number then do the same with each remainder. For instance, converting decimal 53 to binary:

1×2^5 (32) is the highest power, leaving 21 remaining
1×2^4 (16) is the highest power, leaving 5 remaining
0×2^3 (8) next highest power will not go, so still 5 remaining
1×2^2 (4) is the highest power, leaving 1 remaining
0×2^1 (2) next highest power will not go, so still 1 remaining
1×2^0 (1) is the next highest power

So 110101 binary is equivalent to 53 decimal.

Binary arithmetic works just like decimal arithmetic, for instance:

```
   010
 + 111
  1001
```

Computer memory is measured in bytes. A kilobyte is 1,024 bytes, calculated as 2^{10}. Similarly, a megabyte is 1,048,576 bytes (2^{20}), a gigabyte is 1,073,741,824 bytes (2^{30}), and so on.

At the very basic level each byte comprises 8 bits. A bit is a Binary digIT being a single 1 or 0 that forms part of a binary number.

With 8 bits in a byte the binary number in a byte can represent any decimal number in the range of 0 to 255. The significance of this is that all 128 characters defined by standard ASCII codes, plus another 128 special characters, can be stored in computer memory as the binary equivalent of their code number.

This explains why, when a char data-type variable is declared in a C program, the machine allocates a byte of memory for storage.

Binary & hexadecimal

Converting from hexadecimal to binary

This is made very simple by virtue of the fact that each number in the range of 0 to 15 (0 to F in hexadecimal) can be represented as a four-bit binary number.

Each binary equivalent for 0 to 15 (0 to F) is listed in this table:

0 = 0000	4 = 0100	8 = 1000	12(0xC) = 1100
1 = 0001	5 = 0101	9 = 1001	13(0xD) = 1101
2 = 0010	6 = 0110	10(0xA) = 1010	14(0xE) = 1110
3 = 0011	7 = 0111	11(0xB) = 1011	15(0xF) = 1111

Hot tip

The prefix 0x (zero x) denotes a hexadecimal number.

To convert any hexadecimal value to binary just replace each individual number with its binary equivalent.

For instance, converting 0x21F to binary:

```
2 = 0010
1 = 0001
F = 1111  (15)
```

So the hexadecimal value 0x21F is binary 001000011111.

Converting from binary to hexadecimal

As with the technique above this process recognizes that each four-bit binary number can represent a hexadecimal value. To convert a binary number to hexadecimal, starting at the right, split it into groups of 4-bit numbers. Then replace each group with its hexadecimal equivalent.

For instance, converting 11010101011 to hexadecimal:

(0)110 1010 1011 – add an initial zero to make the first group.

```
0110 = 6
1010 = A
1011 = B
```

So the binary number 11010101011 is hexadecimal 0x6AB.

Bitwise AND operator

The C language has six bitwise operators that can be used to perform calculations with binary digits (bits). To appreciate how they are used it is necessary to understand how to convert decimal numbers to binary numbers, as described on page 83.

The bitwise & AND operator resembles the logical && AND operator inasmuch that it requires two operands. Unlike the && operator, which only returns a value of either 1 or 0, the bitwise & operator returns a variety of numbers.

With bitwise & AND the operator compares each individual bit of a binary number and returns a 1 or 0 for each comparison. The end result is a series of ones and zeroes that are converted to their decimal number equivalent.

For instance, take the example 13 & 7. First these decimal operands can be converted to their binary equivalents for bit comparison:

```
13 = 1101 ( (1 x 8) + (1 x 4) + (0 x 2) + (1 x 1) )

7  = 0111 ( (0 x 8) + (1 x 4) + (1 x 2) + (1 x 1) )
```

Starting with the right-hand column each top bit value can now be compared with the corresponding bit value beneath it. If both bits have a value of 1 the & AND operator returns 1 for that part of the comparison, otherwise it returns 0 for that part. In this case, both top and bottom bit values in the right-hand column are 1, so the operator returns 1 for that comparison:

```
        1101
    &   0111
           1
```

The & AND operator continues making comparisons across each pair of bit values until it completes those in the left-hand column:

```
        1101
    &   0111
        0101
```

Converting the result of this example, 0101, back to decimal reveals that 13 & 7 returns 5 ((0 x 8)+(1 x 4)+(0 x 2)+(1 x 1)).

Beware

Don't confuse the logical && operator with the bitwise & operator.

Don't forget

The bitwise & comparison only returns a 1 in the resulting bit value when both compared bit values are 1 – a zero and one comparison returns a zero bit value, also comparing two zeros returns a zero bit value.

Bitwise OR operator

Like the bitwise & AND operator the bitwise | OR operator requires two operands. The | OR operator works in a similar way too, but produces a different result.

The bitwise & operator will only return a bit value of 1 when both operands are themselves 1, whereas the bitwise | OR operator will return a bit value of 1 if either operand is 1.

Hot tip

The | character is commonly known as the "pipe" symbol.

Consequently the bitwise | OR operator will only return a bit value of zero when both operands have a value of zero.

For instance, take the example 10 | 9. First these decimal operands can be converted to their binary equivalents for bit comparison:

```
10 = 1010 ( (1 x 8) + (0 x 4) + (1 x 2) + (0 x 1) )

9  = 1001 ( (1 x 8) + (0 x 4) + (0 x 2) + (1 x 1) )
```

Starting with the right-hand column each top bit value can now be compared with the corresponding bit value beneath it. If both bits have a value of 0 the | OR operator returns 0 for that part of the comparison, otherwise it returns 1 for that part. In this case, both top and bottom bit values in the right-hand column are not 0, so the operator returns 1 for that comparison:

```
        1010
|       1001
           1
```

The | OR operator continues making comparisons across each pair of bit values until it completes those in the left-hand column:

```
        1010
|       1001
        1011
```

Converting the result of this example, 1011, back to decimal reveals that 10 | 9 returns 11 ((1 x 8)+(0 x 4)+(1 x 2)+(1 x 1)).

The bitwise | OR operator should not be confused with the bitwise ^ XOR operator described on the opposite page.

Bitwise XOR operator

Like the bitwise & AND operator and the bitwise | OR operator the bitwise ^ XOR operator (eXclusive OR) also requires two operands. The ^ XOR operator works in a similar way to the | OR operator but is subtly different.

The bitwise | OR operator will return a bit value of 1 when one or both operands are themselves 1, but the bitwise ^ XOR operator will only return a bit value of 1 if just one operand is 1.

Consequently the bitwise ^ XOR operator will return a bit value of zero when both operands have a value of zero, or when both operands have a value of 1.

For instance, take the example 14 ^ 8. First these decimal operands can be converted to their binary equivalents for bit comparison, like this:

```
14 = 1110 ( (1 x 8) + (1 x 4) + (1 x 2) + (0 x 1) )

8  = 1000 ( (1 x 8) + (0 x 4) + (0 x 2) + (0 x 1) )
```

Starting with the right-hand column each top bit value can now be compared with the corresponding bit value beneath it. If just one bit has a value of 1 the ^ XOR operator returns 1 for that part of the comparison, otherwise it returns 0 for that part. In this case, both top and bottom bit values in the right-hand column are 0, so the operator returns 0 for that comparison:

```
        1110
  ^     1000
        ____
           0
```

The ^ XOR operator continues making comparisons across each pair of bit values until it completes those in the left-hand column:

```
        1110
  ^     1000
        ____
        0110
```

Converting the result of this example, 0110, back to decimal reveals that 14 ^ 8 returns 6 ((0 x 8)+(1 x 4)+(1x 2)+(0 x 1)).

Remember that the "X" in XOR stands for "exclusive", to avoid confusion with the | OR operator.

Hot tip

The ^ character is commonly known as the "hat" symbol – typically found on the 6+shift key.

Bitwise NOT operator

bitlogic.c

Unlike the bitwise & AND operator, | OR operator and ^ XOR operator the bitwise ~ NOT operator requires just one operand. It converts the value of this single operand to a binary number then reverses each of its bit values – so all ones become zeroes, and all the zeroes become ones. The bitwise ~ NOT operator then converts the new binary number to decimal and returns that value.

The value returned by the bitwise ~ NOT operator can best be assigned to a unsigned short int variable to be assured that it will be a positive value in the range 0 to 65535.

When considering the arithmetic performed by the ~ NOT operator it is important to use the full 16-digit binary number.

For instance, using the ~ NOT operator on a decimal value of 15:

```
15 = 0000 0000 0000 1111 (  (1x8)+(1x4)+(1x2)+(1x1)  )

~15 = 1111 1111 1111 0000 (65535 - 15 = 65520)
```

This ~ NOT calculation and those for the previous & AND, | OR and ^ XOR examples are demonstrated in this program:

```c
#include <stdio.h>

int main()
{
  unsigned short int num= ~15, unNOT= ~num;
  printf("num = ~15 = %d, ~num = %d\n", num, unNOT);
  printf("14 ^ 8 = %d\n", 14^8 );
  printf("10 | 9 = %d\n", 10|9 );
  printf("13 & 7 = %d\n", 13&7 );
  return 0;
}
```

```
Command Prompt                                    _ □ ✕

C:\MyPrograms>gcc bitlogic.c -o bitlogic.exe

C:\MyPrograms>bitlogic
num = ~15 = 65520, ~num = 15
14 ^ 8 = 6
10 | 9 = 11
13 & 7 = 5

C:\MyPrograms>
```

Setting bit flags

A common use for bitwise operators is to combine several values in a single variable for efficiency. For instance, a program with several "flag" variables, which always have a value of either 1 or 0 (representing true or false states), would normally require eight bits of memory each. The storage of a single digit only requires a single bit, however, so up to eight flags can be combined in a single variable, as seen with the "state" variable in this example:

```c
#include <stdio.h>

#define FLAG_1     1      /* 0000 0001 */
#define FLAG_2     2      /* 0000 0010 */
#define FLAG_3     4      /* 0000 0100 */
#define FLAG_4     8      /* 0000 1000 */
#define FLAG_5     16     /* 0001 0000 */
#define FLAG_6     32     /* 0010 0000 */
#define FLAG_7     64     /* 0100 0000 */
#define FLAG_8     128    /* 1000 0000 */

int main()
{
  int state = 44;         /* 0010 1100 */

  if ((state & FLAG_1) > 0) printf("Flag 1 is set\n");
  if ((state & FLAG_2) > 0) printf("Flag 2 is set\n");
  if ((state & FLAG_3) > 0) printf("Flag 3 is set\n");
  if ((state & FLAG_4) > 0) printf("Flag 4 is set\n");
  if ((state & FLAG_5) > 0) printf("Flag 5 is set\n");
  if ((state & FLAG_6) > 0) printf("Flag 6 is set\n");
  if ((state & FLAG_7) > 0) printf("Flag 7 is set\n");
  if ((state & FLAG_8) > 0) printf("Flag 8 is set\n");
  return 0;
}
```

flags.c

Hot tip

The flag constants have values of increasing powers of 2 to represent individual binary numbers which do not overlap. The state variable value contains an integer total of those flags which are set. For instance, if the state value is 1, flag 1 is set, if the state value is 3, both flags 1 and 2 are set, etc..

```
Command Prompt                                    _ □ ✗
C:\MyPrograms>gcc flags.c -o flags.exe

C:\MyPrograms>flags
Flag 3 is set
Flag 4 is set
Flag 6 is set

C:\MyPrograms>▁
```

Bitwise shift operators

Bitwise left-shift operator

The << left-shift operator converts an integer to a binary number then shifts the bits a specified number of places to the left. It fills the vacated bits with zeros then returns the new value as an integer.

Bits that are shifted beyond the left limit of the variable container simply fall off the edge and are lost.

The example below begins by shifting the bits one place at a time. Then they are shifted further left so that the significant bit (1) moves to the extreme left of the 16-bit unsigned short int variable. The final shift left loses the significant bit altogether.

shiftleft.c

```c
#include <stdio.h>

int main()
{
unsigned short int num = 1;   /* 0000 0000 0000 0001 */

    printf("Number is %d\n",num);
    num = num << 1;              /* 0000 0000 0000 0010 */
    printf("Number is %d\n",num);
    num = num << 1;              /* 0000 0000 0000 0100 */
    printf("Number is %d\n",num);
    num = num << 13;             /* 1000 0000 0000 0000 */
    printf("Number is %d\n",num);
    num = num << 1;          /* (1) 0000 0000 0000 0000 */
    printf("Number is %d\n",num);
    return 0;
}
```

```
C:\MyPrograms>gcc shiftleft.c -o shiftleft.exe

C:\MyPrograms>shiftleft
Number is 5
Number is 10
Number is 20
Number is 32768
Number is 0

C:\MyPrograms>
```

Bitwise right-shift operator

The >> right-shift operator converts an integer to a binary number then shifts its bits a specified number of places to the right. It fills the vacated bits with zeros then returns the new value as an integer.

This works like the << left-shift operator but now bits that are shifted beyond the right limit of the variable container fall off the edge and are lost.

The following example shifts the bits right until the significant bit (1) is shifted beyond the extreme right when it becomes lost.

```c
#include <stdio.h>

int main()
{

unsigned short int num = 2048;  /*0000 1000 0000 0000*/

  printf("Number is %d\n",num);
  num = num >> 4;               /* 0000 0000 1000 0000 */
  printf("Number is %d\n",num);
  num = num >> 4;               /* 0000 0000 0000 1000 */
  printf("Number is %d\n",num);
  num = num >> 3;               /* 0000 0000 0000 0001 */
  printf("Number is %d\n",num);
  num = num >> 1;        /* 0000 0000 0000 0000 (1)*/
  printf("Number is %d\n",num);
  return 0;
}
```

shiftright.c

Don't forget

Shifting right has the effect of dividing the number by 2 for each place shifted.

```
Command Prompt                                    _ □ ✕
C:\MyPrograms>gcc shiftright.c -o shiftright.exe    ▲

C:\MyPrograms>shiftright
Number is 2048
Number is 128
Number is 8
Number is 1
Number is 0

C:\MyPrograms>_                                     ▼
◄                                                ► /
```

Extracting bit values

Another use for bitwise operators is to accomplish particular arithmetical tasks. For instance, imagine a 32-bit integer representing a color with 1 byte (8-bits) each for alpha transparency, red, green and blue values. The single value of, say, the red component can be extracted by a bitwise mask, like this:

```
Color:    AAAA AAAA  RRRR RRRR  GGGG GGGG  BBBB BBBB
Mask:  &  0000 0000  1111 1111  0000 0000  0000 0000
Result:   0000 0000  RRRR RRRR  0000 0000  0000 0000
```

The zeros in this mask use the bitwise & AND operator to ignore all except the red component bits. Binary numbers cannot be used directly in the C code but this mask can be simply stated in hexadecimal form as 0x00FF0000.

The result of this & AND operation leaves the red component value followed by trailing zeros from the green and blue values. Using the >> right-shift operator to shift the red component 16 places to the right leaves the red component completely isolated.

extract.c

```c
#include <stdio.h>

int main()
{
    int color = 0x00CD5C5C;
    int mask  = 0x00FF0000;

    int red = color & mask;
    red = red >> 16;
    printf("Color indianred is %X\n", color );
    printf("Red component of indianred is %X\n", red );
    return 0;
}
```

Hot tip

This example assigns the hexadecimal value of the standard HTML color "indianred" to the variable named color. The bitwise operators simply extract the hexadecimal value of the red component from that color.

```
Command Prompt                                    _ □ ×

C:\MyPrograms>gcc extract.c -o extract.exe

C:\MyPrograms>extract
Colour indianred is CD5C5C
Red component of indianred is CD

C:\MyPrograms>
```

8 Pointing to data

This chapter introduces the "pointer" object and demonstrates how data may be referenced by pointing to the machine address at which that data is stored.

The addressof operator

The & addressof operator was introduced on page 21 in the example demonstrating how to assign input to a variable with the scanf() function. Recall that it must precede the name of the variable name in the call to scanf(), as seen in this code fragment:

```
char letter;

scanf("%c", &letter);
```

Don't forget

The format specifier for a machine address is %p.

When a variable is declared, space is reserved in the machine's memory to store data assigned to that variable. The number of bytes reserved depends upon the data type of the variable. The allotted memory is referenced by the unique variable name.

Envisage the computer's memory as a very long row of slots. Each slot has a unique address, which is expressed in hexadecimal format. It's like a long road of houses – each house contains people and has a unique number, in decimal format. In C programs, the houses are slots and the people are the variables.

The & addressof operator can be used to return the memory address of any variable in hexadecimal format. The example below displays the machine address of an int type variable:

addressof.c

```c
#include <stdio.h>

int main()
{
  int num;
  printf("The num variable is at 0x%p\n", &num);
  return 0;
}
```

```
Command Prompt                                    _ □ ✕
C:\MyPrograms>gcc addressof.c -o addressof.exe

C:\MyPrograms>addressof
The num variable is at 0x0022FF8C

C:\MyPrograms>_
```

L-values and R-values

Once memory space has been reserved by a variable declaration a value of the appropriate data type can be stored there using the = assignment operator.

For instance, num=100 takes the value on the right (100) and puts it in the memory referenced by the variable named num.

The value to the left of the = assignment operator is known as the "L-value" and the value to its right is known as the "R-value". The "L" in L-value can be considered to mean "location" and the "R" in R-value can be considered to mean "read".

One important rule in C programming is that a R-value cannot appear on the left-hand side of the = assignment operator. On the other hand, a L-value may appear on either side of the = assignment operator. Code that breaks this rule, like the example below, will not be compiled.

```c
#include <stdio.h>

int main()
{

  int num; char letter; float decimal; double longer;

  /* These are unacceptable assignment expressions */
  /* as R-values cannot appear on the left of the =  */
  100 = num;
  'A' = letter;
  0.123456 = decimal;
  0.0123456789 = longer;

  return 0;
}
```

values.c

Hot tip

L-values are objects whereas R-values are data.

```
C:\>  Command Prompt                          _ □ ✕

C:\MyPrograms>gcc values.c -o values.exe
values.c: In function `main':
values.c:9: invalid lvalue in assignment
values.c:10: invalid lvalue in assignment
values.c:11: invalid lvalue in assignment
values.c:12: invalid lvalue in assignment

C:\MyPrograms>_
```

Introducing pointers

Pointers are a very useful part of efficient C programming. They are variables that store the memory address of other variables.

Pointer variables are declared in just the same way that other variables are declared but the variable name is prefixed by a "*". In this case, it represents the "dereference operator", and merely denotes that the declared variable is a pointer. The pointer's data type must match the data type of the variable it points to.

Once declared, a pointer variable can be assigned the address of another variable using the & addressof operator. The variable name should not be prefixed by the * dereference operator in the assignment statement unless the pointer is initialized immediately in the variable declaration itself.

Don't forget

Declare variables before making other statements – for instance, at the beginning of main().

- A pointer variable name, when used alone, references a memory address expressed in hexadecimal

The example below declares and initializes a pointer named x_ptr. A second pointer, named y_ptr, is declared then initialized later.

point.c

```c
#include <stdio.h>

int main()
{
  int x = 8, y = 16;

  int *x_ptr = &x;   /* declare & initialize pointer */
  int *y_ptr;    /* declare another pointer variable */
  y_ptr = &y;    /* assign an address to the pointer */
  printf("Address of x: 0x%p\n", x_ptr);
  printf("Address of y: 0x%p\n", y_ptr);
  return 0;
}
```

```
C:\MyPrograms>gcc point.c -o point.exe

C:\MyPrograms>point
Address of x: 0x0022FF8C
Address of y: 0x0022FF88

C:\MyPrograms>
```

Getting values via pointers

When the * dereference operator is used in a variable declaration it merely indicates that the variable being declared is a pointer.

However, when a * dereference operator appears before a pointer variable elsewhere in a program it references the data stored at the address assigned to that pointer.

- A pointer variable name, when prefixed by the * dereference operator, references the data stored at the address assigned to that pointer

This means a program can get the address assigned to a pointer variable just by using its name, or it can get the data stored at that address by prefixing its name with the * dereference operator.

The example below builds on the previous example to reveal the data stored at the address assigned to each pointer variable:

```c
#include <stdio.h>

int main()
{
  int x = 8, y = 16;

  int *x_ptr = &x;
  int *y_ptr;
  y_ptr = &y;
  printf("Address of x: 0x%p\n", x_ptr);
  printf("Value of x: %d\n", *x_ptr );
  printf("Address of y: 0x%p\n", y_ptr);
  printf("Value of y: %d\n", *y_ptr );
  return 0;
}
```

deref.c

Hot tip

The * dereference operator is alternatively known as the "indirection" operator.

```
Command Prompt                           _ □ ✕

C:\MyPrograms>gcc deref.c -o deref.exe

C:\MyPrograms>deref
Address of x: 0x0022FF8C
Value of x: 8
Address of y: 0x0022FF88
Value of y: 16

C:\MyPrograms>_
```

Pointer arithmetic

Once a pointer variable has been created with an assigned address it can be reassigned another address or moved using arithmetic.

The ++ increment operator and the -- decrement operator will move the pointer along to the next or previous address for that data type – the larger the data type, the bigger the jump.

Larger jumps can be achieved using the += and -= operators.

In the example below the pointer moves up one place, then again by a further one place, before jumping back down two places:

moveptr.c

```c
#include <stdio.h>

int main()
{
    int nums[] = {1, 2, 3};

    int *ptr = nums;   /* assign 1st element address */
    printf("ptr address= %p, value= %d\n", ptr, *ptr);

    ptr++;              /* move pointer to 2nd element */
    printf("ptr address= %p, value= %d\n", ptr, *ptr);

    ptr++;              /* move pointer to 3rd element */
    printf("ptr address= %p, value= %d\n", ptr, *ptr);

    ptr-=2;             /* move back down to 1st element */
    printf("ptr address= %p, value= %d\n", ptr, *ptr);

    return 0;
}
```

Beware

The *= and /= arithmetical operators cannot be used to move a pointer.

```
Command Prompt                              _ □ ×

C:\MyPrograms>gcc moveptr.c -o moveptr.exe

C:\MyPrograms>moveptr
ptr address= 0022FF8C, value= 1
ptr address= 0022FF88, value= 2
ptr address= 0022FF84, value= 3
ptr address= 0022FF8C, value= 1

C:\MyPrograms>
```

Pointers and arrays

Pointer arithmetic is especially useful with arrays because the elements in an array occupy consecutive memory places.

Assigning just the name of an array to a pointer automatically assigns it the address of the first element. Incrementing the pointer by one moves the pointer along to the next element.

In the following example a pointer is assigned the name of an array called intArr, which assigns the address of its first element to the pointer. A loop then increments the pointer to each element.

```c
#include <stdio.h>

int main()
{
  int intArr[10] = {1,2,3,4,5,6,7,8,9,10};
  int i;
  int *ptr = intArr;     /* shorthand for intArr[0] */

  for ( i = 0; i < 10; i++ )
  {
    printf("Element %d value = %d\n", i, *ptr);
    ptr++;
  }

  return 0;
}
```

arrayptr.c

Hot tip

The name of an array acts like a pointer to its first element.

99

```
Command Prompt                              _ □ ✕

C:\MyPrograms>gcc arrayptr.c -o arrayptr.exe

C:\MyPrograms>arrayptr
Element 0 value = 1
Element 1 value = 2
Element 2 value = 3
Element 3 value = 4
Element 4 value = 5
Element 5 value = 6
Element 6 value = 7
Element 7 value = 8
Element 8 value = 9
Element 9 value = 10

C:\MyPrograms>_
```

Changing variable values

Besides being able to access the value of a variable via a pointer, a pointer can also be used to change the value inside a variable.

Use the variable pointer name preceded by the * dereference operator to assign a new value of the appropriate data type.

In the following example a character array is created with a pointer variable pointing to its first element. The dereferenced pointer is assigned a character which changes the value of the array's first element. The pointer is then moved, using pointer arithmetic, and assigned a character to change the array's fourth element.

modvar.c

```c
#include <stdio.h>

int main()
{
  char *ptr;
  char charArr[5] = {'f','i','r','e','\0'};
  ptr = charArr;          /* point to 1st array element */

  printf("String is %s\n", charArr);

  *ptr = 'w';                    /* change 1st element */
  printf("String is %s\n", charArr);

  ptr +=3;                    /* move along 3 elements */

  *ptr = 'y';                    /* change 4th element */
  printf("String is %s\n", charArr);

  return 0;
}
```

Don't forget

Add the \0 null character to the end of an array of characters to promote it to string status.

```
C:\MyPrograms>gcc modvar.c -o modvar.exe

C:\MyPrograms>modvar
String is fire
String is wire
String is wiry

C:\MyPrograms>
```

Passing pointers to functions

In C programs function arguments pass their data "by value" to a local variable inside the called function. This means that the function is not operating on the original value, but a copy of it. Passing a pointer to the original value instead overcomes this to allow the called function to operate on the original value.

To demonstrate this, the main() function in the example program below creates a local int variable, named num, together with a pointer to its address. In a call to another function, named triple(), the address of the num variable is passed to another pointer. Because this second pointer then also points to the num variable's address it can be used to assign a new value to num.

```c
#include <stdio.h>

void triple(int *ptr);          /* function prototype */

int main()

{
   int num = 5;
   int *ptr = &num;      /* pointer to address of num */

   printf("The num value is %d\n", num);
   triple(ptr);
   printf("The num value is now %d\n", num);
   return 0;
}

void triple(int *number)
{
   *number = (*number * 3);  /* change the num value */
}
```

passptr.c

Don't forget

Notice that the pointer argument must be included in the function prototype declaration.

```
Command Prompt                                    _ □ ✕
C:\MyPrograms>gcc passptr.c -o passptr.exe

C:\MyPrograms>passptr
The num value is 5
The num value is now 15

C:\MyPrograms>_
```

Arrays of pointers

A C program can contain arrays of pointers in which each element of an array contains the address of another variable.

In the example below five pointers contain the address of individual elements of an int array. A pointer array called ptrs assigns the addresses to its five elements. The address of each of its elements, and the value stored there, is displayed by a for loop.

arrintptrs.c

```
#include <stdio.h>

int main()
{

  int intArr[5] = {1,2,3,4,5};      /* an array of ints */

  int *ptr0 = &intArr[0];      /* address of intArr[0] */
  int *ptr1 = &intArr[1];      /* address of intArr[1] */
  int *ptr2 = &intArr[2];      /* address of intArr[2] */
  int *ptr3 = &intArr[3];      /* address of intArr[3] */
  int *ptr4 = &intArr[4];      /* address of intArr[4] */

  /* an array containing all 5 pointers */
  int *ptrs[5] = { ptr0, ptr1, ptr2, ptr3, ptr4 };

  int i;

for( i = 0; i < 5; i++ )
{
printf("The value at 0x%p is %d\n", ptrs[i],*ptrs[i]);
}

  return 0;
}
```

Hot tip

Notice how the value of the counter "i" is substituted for the element index number on each iteration of the loop.

```
C:\MyPrograms>gcc arrintptrs.c -o arrintptrs.exe

C:\MyPrograms>arrintptrs
The value at 0x0022FF68 is 1
The value at 0x0022FF6C is 2
The value at 0x0022FF70 is 3
The value at 0x0022FF74 is 4
The value at 0x0022FF78 is 5

C:\MyPrograms>
```

A character array that ends with the \0 null character has string status so can be assigned to a pointer. The name of a string char array acts like a pointer to its first element so the addressof operator is not needed when assigning a string to a pointer.

The program below assigns a single string to a char pointer and three strings to a char pointer array. The address of each element is passed to another function and then their contents displayed.

```c
#include <stdio.h>

void display(char *ptr[]);    /* function prototype */

int main()
{
  char str[9] = {'C',' ','i','s',' ','f','u','n','\0'};
  char *string = str; /* no addressof operator needed*/
  char *strings[3] = { "one", "two", "three" };
  printf("%s\n", string);
  display(strings);
  return 0;
}

void display(char *ptr[])      /* function definition */
{
  int i = 0;

  while ( i < 3 )
  {
    printf("%s\n", ptr[i]);
    i++;
  }
}
```

strptrs.c

103

Hot tip

Notice that the entire string in a char pointer is referenced by the pointer name alone – without the * dereference operator.

Beware

To include a space in a string there must actually be a space between the single quotes, like this ' ' – two single quotes together, such as '' is seen as an empty element and causes a compiler error.

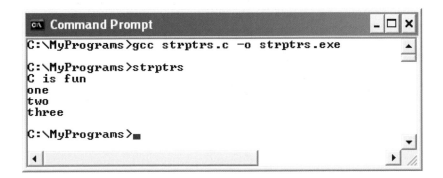

```
Command Prompt                                    - □ ×
C:\MyPrograms>gcc strptrs.c -o strptrs.exe

C:\MyPrograms>strptrs
C is fun
one
two
three

C:\MyPrograms>_
```

Pointing to functions

Pointers can point to functions, although this ability is used less often than pointers that point to data values.

A pointer to a function is like a pointer to data but must always be enclosed in plain brackets when using the * dereference operator to avoid a compiler error. These will be followed by plain brackets containing any arguments to be passed to the function when using the * dereference operator.

This example contains a pointer to a function named add() which takes two arguments and returns an int data type. The pointer declaration must match the number of arguments and return type of the function it points at. The function is called, via the pointer, to return the sum total of two integers passed to it as arguments.

fcnptr.c

```c
#include <stdio.h>

int add(int x, int y);           /* function prototype */

int main()
{
  int (*ptr)(int x, int y);       /* declare pointer */
  int x = 8, y = 16;

  ptr = add;           /* point to the add() function */
  /* now call the add() function via the pointer...*/
  printf("%d plus %d equals %d\n", x, y, (*ptr)(x,y));
  return 0;
}

int add(int x, int y)           /* function definition */
{
  return x+y;
}
```

```
Command Prompt                          _ □ ✕

C:\MyPrograms>gcc fcnptr.c -o fcnptr.exe

C:\MyPrograms>fcnptr
8 plus 16 equals 24

C:\MyPrograms>_
```

9 Manipulating strings

This chapter explores the text "string" object and demonstrates how it may be manipulated in a C program by string functions.

What is a string?

A string of text is a series of characters, usually forming words. In C programming each character has a unique ASCII code value, including punctuation and non-printing characters such as newline and tab. These are used by C to treat characters numerically. For instance, characters can be changed arithmetically like this:

```
char letter = 'S';
letter++;              /* changes the letter to 'T' */
```

The ASCII code values for lowercase letters are always 32 higher than those of uppercase letters, so the case of a character can be changed by adding or subtracting a value of 32:

```
char letter = 'A';
letter += 32;    /* changes the letter to 'a' */
letter -= 32;    /* changes the letter back to 'A' */
```

C does not have a dedicated string data type, but relies instead upon its char data type to store strings as character arrays. A char array to store a string is declared like this:

```
char arr[6];
```

This declaration reserves sufficient memory space to store six characters. Filling each of these six array elements with characters does not create a string however – just an array of characters. The crucial requirement to create a string in this array is that the final element must contain the \0 null character.

The inclusion of a \0 null character in the final element of a character array promotes the array to string status where the entire array is regarded as a "string constant".

In a string constant the name of the array acts as an implied pointer to the entire string of characters, ending with the \0 null character. The sizeof() function will return the size of the string when passed a string's name as its argument. A string may be assigned to a char array or to a char pointer, like this:

```
char arr[6] = {'A','l','p','h','a','\0'};
char *ptr = "Beta";
printf("%s\n", arr);      /* outputs "Alpha" */
printf("%s\n", ptr);      /* outputs "Beta" */
```

Hot tip

Refer to page 162 to see the standard ASCII character code table.

Don't forget

In C, character values must be enclosed by single quotes – strings must be enclosed by double quotes.

Hot tip

There is an example illustrating the assignment of strings to a char array and a char pointer on page 103.

106

The problem with scanf()

The scanf() function was introduced on page 21 as a means of introducing character input from the user. This function works well for single characters or multiple characters forming a single word. The problem is that scanf() stops reading the input when it encounters a single space or when the return key is pressed.

This means that a string sentence cannot be input using scanf() – as soon as a space is input the string ends.

To demonstrate this problem the program below asks the user to enter a string containing spaces. The scanf() function is used to read the input which it assigns to two char arrays. The contents of each array is then displayed to illustrate what scanf() actually recorded:

```c
#include <stdio.h>

int main()
{
  char arr1[50];
  char arr2[50];

  printf("Enter up to 50 characters, with spaces\n");
  scanf("%s", arr1);
  scanf("%s", arr2);
  printf("Input read into 1st array: %s\n", arr1);
  printf("Input read into 2nd array: %s\n", arr2);
  printf("Everything else has been lost\n");
  return 0;
}
```

scanfprob.c

Hot tip

A solution to this problem is provided on the next page.

Reading strings

A solution to the scanf() problem, described on the previous page, lies with two standard functions located in the stdio.h header file.

The first function is named gets() and is used to read input from the user. It can then assign the input string to a char array specified as its argument. Normally when the return key is pressed a non-printing newline character is input. The gets() function replaces this with a \0 null character to ensure that the char array is promoted to string status.

The companion to the gets() function is named puts(). This function will output a string specified as its argument, and add a newline at the end.

Both puts() and gets() are demonstrated in the program below which overcomes the problem in the previous example:

getsputs.c

```
#include <stdio.h>

int main()
{
  char arr[50];

  printf("Enter up to 50 characters, with spaces\n");
  gets(arr);

  printf("\nInput read into array was:\n");
  puts(arr);

  return 0;
}
```

Hot tip

If you don't want a newline added after the output use the printf() function instead of puts() to write the output.

Finding string length

The standard C libraries include a header file named string.h that contains special string-handling functions.

To make these available to a program the string.h header file must be added with an #include directive at the start of the program.

The string.h header file contains a function named strlen() that can be used to discover the length of a string specified as its argument. The returned integer will be the total number of characters in that string not including the \0 null character.

In the following example the strlen() function returns the number of characters in a string that is entered by the user:

```c
#include <stdio.h>

#include <string.h>        /* make strlen() available */

int main()
{
  char arr[50];

  printf("Enter up to 50 characters, with spaces\n");
  gets(arr);
  printf("\nInput read into array is:\n");
  puts(arr);

  printf("String length: %d characters\n",strlen(arr));

  printf("Array size: %d bytes\n", sizeof(arr) );

  return 0;
}
```

strlen.c

Don't forget

In this example the gets() function added a \0 null character in the 11th element of the array – this is not included in the number returned by strlen().

Copying strings

The string.h header file contains two useful functions to copy strings from one array to another. To make these available to a program the string.h header file must be added with an #include directive at the start of the program.

The first string copying function is named strcpy() and it requires two arguments. The first argument specifies the name of the target array to copy the string into, and the second argument specifies the name of the source array from where it should be copied:

strcpy (target-array , source-array) ;

All characters in the source array are copied to the target array including the \0 null terminating character. If there are other elements after the null character these also are padded with \0s. This ensures that remnants of the original longer second string in this example no longer survive after the first string is copied there:

strcpy.c

```c
#include <stdio.h>

#include <string.h>        /* make strcpy() available */

int main ()
{
    char string1[50]= "first string of text";
    char string2[50]= "second (longer) string of text";

    /* copy to string 2 the contents of string1 */
    strcpy(string2, string1);

    printf("1st string contains: %s\n", string1);
    printf("2nd string contains: %s\n", string2);
    return 0;
}
```

Beware

Ensure that the target array is of sufficient size to hold all the characters in the string being copied – including its terminating \0 null character.

```
C:\MyPrograms>gcc strcpy.c -o strcpy.exe

C:\MyPrograms>strcpy
1st string contains: first string of text
2nd string contains: first string of text

C:\MyPrograms>
```

The second string copying function in the string.h header file is named strncpy(). This is used like the strcpy() function but takes a third argument to specify how much of the string to copy.

strncpy (target-array , source-array , length) ;

The string being copied will begin with the first character of the source string but will end at the position specified by this third argument. After the characters have been copied the next element in the target array must receive a terminating \0 null character to promote the character array to string status. Ensure that the target array is always at least one element larger than the number of characters being copied to allow space for a final \0 null character.

The example below copies a string of five characters into an array of ten elements – and string2[5] is assigned a \0 null character:

```c
#include <stdio.h>

#include <string.h>      /* make strncpy() available */

int main ()
{
  char string1[] = "To be or not to be?";
  char string2[10];

  /* copy first 5 characters in string1 to string2 */
  strncpy (string2, string1, 5);
/* add a string terminator in the 6th element */
  string2[5] = '\0';

  printf("1st string: %s\n", string1 );
  printf("2nd string: %s\n", string2 );
  return 0;
}
```

Don't forget

The last element in string2 is number 5 – because array index numbering starts at zero, not one.

strncpy.c

Hot tip

Notice that the size of the first array is not specified but is automatically set because the array is initialized in the declaration. Other arrays that are to be initialized after their declaration, say by user input or copying from other arrays, must specify a size in their declaration.

```
C:\ Command Prompt                                 _ □ ✕

C:\MyPrograms>gcc strncpy.c -o strncpy.exe

C:\MyPrograms>strncpy
1st string: To be or not to be?
2nd string: To be

C:\MyPrograms>_
```

Validating strings

The header file named ctype.h contains a range of standard functions that are useful to perform tests on characters. To make these available to a program the ctype.h header file must be added with an #include directive at the start of the program.

For instance, the isalpha() function determines if the tested character is a letter, the isdigit() function determines if the tested character is a decimal digit and the isalnum() function determines if the tested character is either a letter or a digit.

Each test function returns a non-zero value (not necessarily a 1), if a tested character is as expected but returns a zero if it is not.

These test functions can be used to validate input from a user to check that it conforms to the format expected by the program. In the program below the user is asked to input six digits which are assigned to a char array. Each character is tested in turn to verify that it is indeed a digit. When a non-digit is discovered a call to the printf() function writes out an appropriate message.

Hot tip

Notice how a variable is used as a flag in this example to record the state of validity – it is initialized as true (1) but is set to false (0) when a non-digit is discovered.

isval.c

Don't forget

The test in this case !isdigit() could alternatively be expressed using the code isdigit==0.

```
#include <stdio.h>
#include <ctype.h>        /* make char tests available */

int main()
{
 char string[7];
 char *pos[] = {"1st","2nd","3rd","4th","5th","6th"};
 int i, flag = 1;

 puts("Enter any six numbers without any spaces...");
 gets(string);
 for( i = 0; i < 5; i++ )
 {

  if( !isdigit(string[i]) )
  {
  printf("Non-digit found in the %s entry\n",pos[i] );
  flag = 0;
  }
 }
 (flag) ? puts("Entry valid") : puts("Entry invalid");
 return 0;
}
```

The ctype.h header file also contains functions to test and change character case. This example converts all input to uppercase:

```c
#include <stdio.h>
#include <ctype.h>     /* make char tests available */

int main()
{
  char string[50]; int i;
  puts("Enter some text..."); gets(string);
  for( i = 0; i < 50; i++ )
  {
  if(!isupper(string[i])) string[i]=toupper(string[i]);
  }
  puts(string);
  return 0;
}
```

case.c

Hot tip

There are also islower() and tolower() functions dealing with lowercase characters – the full range of character test functions are given in the Reference section on page 173.

Converting strings

The stdlib.h header file contains a useful function named atoi() that can convert a string to an int data type. To make this available to a program the stdlib.h header file must be added with an #include directive at the start of the program.

The atoi() function takes the string to be converted as its single argument. If the string is empty, or if the string's first character is not a number or a minus sign, then atoi() will return zero. Otherwise the numeric string will be converted to an int data type until atoi() encounters a non-numeric character in the string.

When atoi() meets a non-numeric character in the string it returns the number so far converted as an int data type. The conversion results in the following example demonstrate how atoi() performs the conversion until it meets a non-numeric character:

atoi.c

```c
#include <stdio.h>
#include <stdlib.h>          /* make atoi() available */

int main()
{
   char string1[] = "246eight10";
   char string2[] = "-65.8";
   char *string3 = "x13579";
   int result;

   result = atoi(string1);
   printf("str1: %d\n", result );
   printf("str2: %d\n", atoi(string2) );
   printf("str3: %d\n", atoi(string3) );
   return 0;
}
```

```
C:\ Command Prompt                          _ □ ✕

C:\MyPrograms>gcc atoi.c -o atoi.exe

C:\MyPrograms>atoi
str1: 246
str2: -65
str3: 0

C:\MyPrograms>_
```

There is also a function named itoa() that can be used to convert an int data type to a string. This is widely used but is not part of the standard ANSI specification.

This function requires three arguments to specify the number to be converted, the string to which the converted number is to be assigned, and finally the base to be used for the conversion. For instance, a base of 2 converts the number to a string binary.

An ANSI -compliant alternative to the itoa() function is the sprintf() function that is part of the stdio.h header file. It is less powerful because a base value cannot be specified. It too takes three arguments – to specify the string where the conversion is to be stored, a format specifier and the number to be converted. The function returns the number of characters in the converted string.

```c
#include <stdio.h>
#include <stdlib.h>

int main()
{
  char str[4];
  int i;

  printf("12 in binary is %s\n", itoa(12,str,2));
  printf("12 in hexadecimal is %s\n",itoa(12,str,16));

  i = sprintf(str, "%x", 255);
  printf("255 in hexadecimal is %s\n", str);
  printf("sprintf() returns: %d\n", i);
  return 0;
}
```

Beware

The itoa() function is very useful but because it is not part of the ANSI standard it may not be supported by all compilers – it is supported by the GNU C compiler used in this book.

itoa.c

Command Prompt

```
C:\MyPrograms>gcc itoa.c -o itoa.exe

C:\MyPrograms>itoa
12 in binary is 1100
12 in hexadecimal is c
255 in hexadecimal is ff
sprintf() returns: 2

C:\MyPrograms>
```

Don't forget

Unlike the itoa() function, sprintf() cannot convert to binary because there is no format specifier for binary numbers.

115

String concatenation

The combining of two strings into one single string is more precisely known as string "concatenation".

The string.h header file contains two functions that can be used to combine strings. To make these available to a program the string.h header file must be added with an #include directive at the start of the program.

The first of these functions is named strcat() and it takes the name of two strings to be concatenated as its two arguments. The string named as its second argument is added to that named as its first argument and then the function returns the combined first string.

It is important to note that the first string must be large enough to accommodate all the characters of the concatenated string to avoid a compiler error.

This example concatenates two strings and displays their total size:

strcat.c

```
#include <stdio.h>
#include <string.h>

int main()
{
 char string1[100] = "A place for everything ";
 char string2[30] = "and everything in its place";
 int numchars;

 numchars = (strlen(string1) + strlen(string2));
 printf("string1 must hold %d characters\n",numchars);
 strcat( string1, string2 );
 printf("%s\n", string1);
 return 0;
}
```

Don't forget

The strlen() function returns the length of a string not including the \0 null character – in this case the minimum size of string1 must be 51, not 50.

```
C:\ Command Prompt                              - □ ×
C:\MyPrograms>gcc strcat.c -o strcat.exe

C:\MyPrograms>strcat
string1 must hold 50 characters
A place for everything and everything in its place

C:\MyPrograms>_
```

The second string concatenation function contained in the string.h header file is named strncat(). It is similar to the strcat() function but takes a third argument to specify how many characters of the second string argument should be added to the first string argument.

In the example below the first call to strncat() adds the beginning of the second string onto the first string. A second call to the strncat() function adds the end of the second string onto the first string.

Notice how the position to begin copying the characters is stated using pointer arithmetic – the name of the string is an implied pointer to its first character, so its name +1 points to its second character, and so on.

```c
#include <stdio.h>
#include <string.h>

int main()
{
  char string1[100] = "The truth is rarely pure ";
  char string2[32] = "and never simple. - Oscar Wilde";

/* add the first 17 letters of string 2 to string 1 */
  strncat( string1, string2, 17 );
  printf("%s\n", string1);

/* add the last 14 letters of string 2 to string 1 */
  strncat( string1, (string2 + 17), 14 );
  printf("%s\n", string1);
  return 0;
}
```

strncat.c

```
C:\ Command Prompt                              - □ ×
C:\MyPrograms>gcc strncat.c -o strncat.exe

C:\MyPrograms>strncat
The truth is rarely pure and never simple.
The truth is rarely pure and never simple. - Oscar Wilde

C:\MyPrograms>_
```

Finding substrings

A string can be searched to determine if it contains a specified "substring" sequence of characters with a function named strstr(). This is part of the string.h header file which must be added with an #include directive to make this function available.

The strstr() function takes two arguments – the first is the string to be searched and the second is the substring to seek. If the substring is not found the function returns a NULL value. When the substring is found the function returns a pointer to the first occurrence of the specified substring within the searched string.

The following example twice calls strstr() to search for a substring. The returned pointer in the successful search is used to output the searched string from the point at which it first occurs.

strstr.c

```c
#include <stdio.h>
#include <string.h>

int main()
{
  char *string = "The man who makes no mistakes
                  does not usually make anything";

  printf("%s\n", strstr(string, "woman") );
  if( strstr(string, "woman") == NULL )
    printf("\'woman\' not found in string\n");

  printf("%s\n", strstr(string, "ake"));
  if( strstr(string, "ake") != NULL )
    printf("\'ake\' found in string\n");

  return 0;
}
```

Don't forget

The substring "ake" actually occurs three times in the searched string – but after the first instance is found, the strstr() function just returns a pointer to its first character.

```
C:\MyPrograms>gcc strstr.c -o strstr.exe

C:\MyPrograms>strstr
<null>
'woman' not found in string
akes no mistakes does not usually make anything
'ake' found in string

C:\MyPrograms>
```

The string position of the first character of a located substring can be calculated using pointer arithmetic – the address of the searched string points to its first character. This can be subtracted from the address of the substring's first character that is returned by the strstr() function. The difference reveals the element position of the start of the substring within the searched string.

This calculation is demonstrated in the following program:

```c
#include <stdio.h>
#include <string.h>

int main()
{
  char *str = "No time like the present";
  char *sub = "like";
  char *ptr;    /* pointer for the substring address */
  int   pos;        /* to store the element position */

  ptr = strstr(str,sub);    /* get substring address */

  printf("Address of string \'%s\': 0x%p\n", str,str);
  printf("Address of substring\'%s\': 0x%p\n",sub,ptr);

  pos = (ptr - str);                /* do the arithmetic */

  printf("In decimal, %d - %d = %d\n", ptr, str, pos );
  printf("So the first occurence of %s in\n ", sub);
  printf("\'%s\'\nis at element %d\n", str, pos );
  return 0;
}
```

Don't forget

Element index numbering starts at zero, not one – so element no.8 stores the ninth character.

strstrpos.c

Hot tip

The string.h header file also contains two character functions – strchr() finds the first occurrence of a character in a string, and strrchr() finds its last occurrence – both return NULL if the character is not found.

119

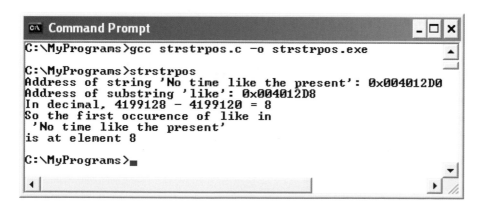

```
Command Prompt                                        _ □ ×
C:\MyPrograms>gcc strstrpos.c -o strstrpos.exe

C:\MyPrograms>strstrpos
Address of string 'No time like the present': 0x004012D0
Address of substring 'like': 0x004012D8
In decimal, 4199128 - 4199120 = 8
So the first occurence of like in
 'No time like the present'
is at element 8

C:\MyPrograms>_
```

Comparing strings

In C programming the == and != comparison operators cannot be used to compare strings. Instead, the string.h header file contains a function named strcmp() which can be used for that purpose. To use this function the string.h header file must be added with an #include directive at the start of the program.

The strcmp() function takes the name of two strings to be compared as its two arguments. The comparison is made based upon the numerical value and position of each string character. When the strings are identical strcmp() returns zero, otherwise it returns a positive or negative integer depending on the string values. This is demonstrated in the example below which shows that strcmp() recognizes that "abc" and "cab" are not identical:

strcmp.c

```c
#include <stdio.h>
#include <string.h>

int main()
{
  char *string[4] = { "abc", "xyz", "cab", "abc" } ;
  int result;

  result = strcmp( string[0], string[1] );
  printf("Result comparing abc to xyz is %d\n",result);
  result = strcmp( string[1], string[0] );
  printf("Result comparing xyz to abc is %d\n",result);
  result = strcmp( string[0], string[2] );
  printf("Result comparing abc to cab is %d\n",result);
  result = strcmp( string[0], string[3] );
  printf("Result comparing abc to abc is %d\n",result);
  return 0;
}
```

Hot tip

The strcmp() comparison is case-sensitive – for instance, "ABC" and "abc" are not seen as equal. Comparisons are based on the characters' ASCII values where 'A' is 65 and 'a' is 97 so will not be found equal.

```
Command Prompt                                    _ □ ✗
C:\MyPrograms>gcc strcmp.c -o strcmp.exe

C:\MyPrograms>strcmp
Result comparing abc to xyz is -1
Result comparing xyz to abc is 1
Result comparing abc to cab is -1
Result comparing abc to abc is 0

C:\MyPrograms>▮
```

10 Building structures

This chapter introduces the "struct" (structure) and "union" abstract data types and demonstrates how they may be used in a C program to group together multiple variables of different type.

What is a structure?

A structure in a C program can contain one, or more, variables of the same, or different data types. These are grouped together in a single structure and can be conveniently referenced using its name.

Grouping related variables together in a structure is helpful in organizing complicated data, especially in large programs. For instance, a structure might be created to describe a payroll record, with variables to store an employee's name, address, salary, national insurance number, etc..

Where arrays can be used to store items of data of the same data type, structures can store items of data of various data types. Each variable in an array is called an "element", but each variable in a structure is called a "member". Individual elements of an array are accessed by their index number (inside square brackets), individual members of a structure are accessed by their given name.

The "struct" keyword is used to declare a structure in a C program and is followed by an optional "tag" name for that structure. All the variable members of the structure are then listed within a pair of braces – these can include arrays and pointers.

A struct containing members to describe the x, y coordinate values of a point in a graph could be declared like this:

```
struct coords
{
    int x;
    int y;
};
```

The struct declaration defines a new data type and variables of that data type can be declared in the same way that int, char, float and double variables are declared. For instance, a variable named "point" of the data type "coords" can be declared like this:

```
struct coords
{
    int x;
    int y;
} point;
```

Beware

Variable members of a structure cannot be initialized in the declaration.

Don't forget

Notice the semi-colon after the struct declaration.

Hot tip

Multiple variables can be declared in a struct declaration if separated by a comma – as with regular data types.

Each struct member can be addressed by appending the "."
dot operator and the member's name to the variable name. For
instance, the members in the struct declaration above can be
addressed as point.x and point.y.

Also, a new struct can be declared using the tag name of an
existing struct. This new struct inherits the original member
properties. For instance, the declaration below creates a struct
named "top", based on the struct named "coords", with variables
top.x and top.y.

```
struct coords top;
```

The following program demonstrates the examples given above
and illustrates how to access the struct members:

```
#include <stdio.h>

struct coords
{
   int x;
   int y;
} point;

struct coords top;

int main()
{
   point.x = 5; point.y = 8;
   top.x = 16;   top.y = 27;
   printf("point x:%d, point y:%d\n", point.x,point.y);
   printf("top x:%d, top y:%d\n", top.x, top.y);
   return 0;
}
```

struct.c

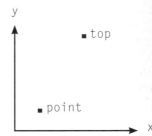

123

```
C:\MyPrograms>gcc struct.c -o struct.exe

C:\MyPrograms>struct
point x:5, point y:8
top x:16, top y:27

C:\MyPrograms>
```

Defining type structures

A data type defined by a struct can be declared to be a type definition by adding the typedef keyword at the beginning of the struct declaration. This identifies that struct to be a prototype from which other structs can be created simply using any of its declared variable names – without the struct keyword.

The program listed below builds on the example given on the previous page to demonstrate how the struct named "coords" can be promoted to a type definition. From this two further structs are created using its declared variable named "point". Notice that these struct declarations can optionally initialize all their variables as a comma-separated list within braces.

typestruct.c

Beware

The struct can only assign a list of values to all its variables using this technique in its declaration – not later in the program.

```c
#include <stdio.h>

typedef struct coords
{
   int x;
   int y;
} point;

point top;
point btm = {2,15};

int main()
{
   top.x = 16;
   top.y = 27;
   printf("top x:%d, top y:%d\n", top.x, top.y);
   printf("bottom x:%d bottom y: %d\n", btm.x, btm.y);
   return 0;
}
```

```
Command Prompt                                    _ □ ✕

C:\MyPrograms>gcc typestruct.c -o typestruct.exe

C:\MyPrograms>typestruct
top x:16, top y:27
bottom x:2 bottom y: 15

C:\MyPrograms>
```

Nesting structures

A struct may be nested inside another struct. The example to demonstrate this creates a struct to record the x, y coordinates of two points, representing diagonally opposing corners of a rectangle.

Individual struct members are now accessed using two dot operators, following the syntax *outer-struct.inner-struct.member*

```c
#include <stdio.h>

struct coords
{
  int x;
  int y;
};

struct rect
{
  struct coords pt1;
  struct coords pt2;
};

struct rect box;

int main()
{
  box.pt1.x = 5;
  box.pt1.y = 10;
  box.pt2.x = 25;
  box.pt2.y = 25;
  printf("Point 1 x: %d, y: %d\n",box.pt1.x,box.pt1.y);
  printf("Point 2 x: %d, y: %d\n",box.pt2.x,box.pt2.y);
  return 0;
}
```

neststruct.c

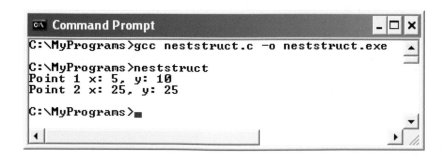

Command Prompt

```
C:\MyPrograms>gcc neststruct.c -o neststruct.exe

C:\MyPrograms>neststruct
Point 1 x: 5, y: 10
Point 2 x: 25, y: 25

C:\MyPrograms>_
```

Hot tip

All four variable values could alternatively be assigned in the declaration of the rect box struct using struct rect box = {5,10,25,25}.

Arrays & pointers in structs

There is an advantage in using a char pointer in a struct as a string container over using a char array for the same purpose.

An entire string can only be assigned to a char array when it is declared. The only way to subsequently assign a string to a struct char array is one element at a time, because individual elements of the array are L-values. A char pointer is also a L-value so it can be assigned an entire string after it has been declared.

This example creates a struct with both types of char members and illustrates the difference in how they may subsequently be assigned string values.

arrvptr.c

Don't forget

All char array variables are R-values – so cannot appear on the left in an = assignment expression. Their elements, on the other hand, can do because they are L-values.

```c
#include <stdio.h>

struct example
{
  char arr_string[4];
  char *ptr_string;
} str;

int main()
{
  str.arr_string[0] = 'b';
  str.arr_string[1] = 'a';
  str.arr_string[2] = 'd';
  str.arr_string[3] = '\0';
  str.ptr_string = "good";
  printf("The array string is %s\n", str.arr_string );
  printf("The pointer string is %s\n",str.ptr_string);
  return 0;
}
```

```
C:\MyPrograms>gcc arrvptr.c -o arrvptr.exe

C:\MyPrograms>arrvptr
The array string is bad
The pointer string is good

C:\MyPrograms>
```

Pointing to structures

Pointers can be created to struct data types just as they can with regular data types. The use of pointers to structures is so common in C programs that there is even a special operator to describe it.

In a struct pointer the "." dot operator can be replaced by "->", which is a hyphen followed by the greater-than character.

The following example demonstrates the creation of a struct pointer and illustrates how the -> arrow operator is used in place of the dot operator:

```c
#include <stdio.h>

typedef struct coords    /* create a point data type */
{
   int x;
   int y;
} point;

int main()
{
   point pt1;        /* create a struct of type point */
   point *pt2;    /*create struct pointer of type point*/

   pt1.x = 5;      /* assign values to struct members */
   pt1.y = 10;

   pt2 = &pt1;    /* assign pointer address of struct */

   printf("Starting point %d %d\n",pt1.x, pt2->y );
   printf("Coordinate x: %d, y: %d\n", pt2->x, pt1.y);
   return 0;
}
```

structptr.c

Hot tip

The -> arrow operator is useful in C programming to differentiate between structure pointers and other pointers.

```
Command Prompt                                    _ □ ✕
C:\MyPrograms>gcc structptr.c -o structptr.exe

C:\MyPrograms>structptr
Starting point 5 10
Coordinate x: 5, y: 10

C:\MyPrograms>_
```

Arrays of structures

Structure member values can be stored in an array, just like the values of any other data type.

The array is declared as usual but the method used to assign values to its elements is slightly different. Each comma-separated list of member values must be enclosed by its own pair of braces.

The example below creates an array with three elements of the point data type, which contains two members. The array elements are initialized in the declaration with a value given to each member in each element. Subsequently new values are assigned to the members of the third element:

arrstruct.c

```c
#include <stdio.h>

typedef struct coords
{
   int x;
   int y;
} point;

int main()
{
   point pts[3] = { {4,8}, {5,10}, {16,27} };
   pts[2].x = 18;
   pts[2].y = 25;

   printf("Point 0 x: %d, y: %d\n",pts[0].x,pts[0].y );
   printf("Point 1 x: %d, y: %d\n",pts[1].x,pts[1].y );
   printf("Point 2 x: %d, y: %d\n",pts[2].x,pts[2].y );
   return 0;
}
```

Beware

Simply assigning all the values as a single comma-separated list will not work – each set of values must be enclosed by its own pair of braces.

```
Command Prompt                                    _ □ ✕

C:\MyPrograms>gcc arrstruct.c -o arrstruct.exe

C:\MyPrograms>arrstruct
Point 0 x: 4, y: 8
Point 1 x: 5, y: 10
Point 2 x: 18, y: 25

C:\MyPrograms>_
```

Passing structs to functions

A structure can be passed as an argument to a function by first specifying the struct data type, and a variable name, in the function prototype declaration. Structures of the named type can then be passed to the function named in the prototype declaration. This example passes two point type structs to a function named display():

```c
#include <stdio.h>

typedef struct coords    /* create a point data type */
{
  int x;
  int y;
} point;

void display( point pt );      /* function prototype */

int main()
{
  point pt1, pt2;    /* create structs of type point */
  pt1.x = 8;                    /* assign member values */
  pt1.y = 16;
  pt2.x = 5;
  pt2.y = 10;

  display( pt1 );          /* pass structs to function */
  display( pt2 );
  return 0;
}

void display( point pt )
{
  printf("Point x: %d, y: %d\n", pt.x, pt.y);
}
```

passstruct.c

Hot tip

Pointers to structures can also be passed to functions by first including them in the function prototype declaration. For instance: void display(point *pt);

```
Command Prompt                                      _ □ ✕
C:\MyPrograms>gcc passstruct.c -o passstruct.exe    ▲

C:\MyPrograms>passstruct
Point x: 8, y: 16
Point x: 5, y: 10

C:\MyPrograms>_                                      ▼
◄ |                                                | ► |
```

What is a union?

In C programming a "union" allows different pieces of data, of any data type, to be stored at the same memory locations as the program proceeds – assigning a value to the union will overwrite that previously stored there. This allows efficient use of memory.

A union is like a struct but is declared with the "union" keyword and, because of its nature, its member values can only be assigned individually. This example demonstrates the difference between a struct and a union and shows how union values are overwritten:

union.c
(part of)

Don't forget

It is the programmer's responsibility to understand which type of data is being stored in a union at any point in the execution of the program.

```c
#include <stdio.h>

typedef struct data1    /* create a struct of type s */
{
    int num1;
    int num2;
    char letter;
    char *string;
} s;

typedef union data2     /* create a union of type u */
{
    int num1;
    int num2;
    char letter;
    char *string;
} u;

int main()
{
    s sdata = { 10, 20,'C',"Programs" };
    u udata;

/* display value and address of each struct member */

    printf("\nsdata.num1: %d ", sdata.num1 );
    printf("\t\tstored at: 0x%p\n", &sdata.num1 );
    printf("sdata.num2: %d ", sdata.num2 );
    printf("\t\tstored at: 0x%p\n", &sdata.num2 );
    printf("sdata.letter: %c ", sdata.letter );
    printf("\tstored at: 0x%p\n", &sdata.letter );
    printf("sdata.string: %s ", sdata.string );
    printf("\tstored at: 0x%p\n", &sdata.string );
```

```c
/* assign a value to each union member in turn then */
/* display value and address of each union member   */

  udata.num1 = 8;
  printf("\nudata.num1: %d ", udata.num1 );
  printf("\t\tstored at: 0x%p\n", &udata.num1 );
  udata.num2 = 16;
  printf("udata.num2: %d ", udata.num2 );
  printf("\t\tstored at: 0x%p\n", &udata.num2 );
  udata.letter = 'A';
  printf("udata.letter: %c ", udata.letter );
  printf("\tstored at: 0x%p\n", &udata.letter );
  udata.string = "Union";
  printf("udata.string: %s ", udata.string );
  printf("\tstored at: 0x%p\n", &udata.string );

  /* show the original value is overwritten */
  printf("\nudata.num1 is now: %d ", udata.num1 );
  printf("overwritten by \"Union\"\n");

  return 0;
}
```

union.c
(continued)

Hot tip

Unions are mostly useful when memory is very limited.

131

The memory address of each struct member is seen to be unique – but the single memory address of the union is shared by all its members:

Arrays of unions

An array of unions can be created in the same way as an array of structures were created in the example on page 128. The difference with unions is that its members cannot be initialized in a declaration unless all members are of the same data type. Given the purpose of unions this is unlikely, so each member must be initialized individually by referencing its array index number.

The example below creates an array of three unions which are then individually assigned member values:

arrunion.c

Hot tip

The data type of the first member in a union is recognized by the compiler as the default type for that union – in this case it's the char data type. So the array of unions in this example could be initialized in its declaration with the assignment of ={"one","two","three"};

```c
#include <stdio.h>

/* declare a union of type uniondata */
typedef union data
{
  char *fname;
  char *lname;
  int age;
} uniondata;

int main()
{
  uniondata toon[3];    /* create an array of unions */
  /*but can't initialize with ={"Mickey","Mouse",75};*/

  toon[0].fname = "Mickey";    /* initialize elements */
  toon[1].lname = "Mouse";
  toon[2].age = 75;

  printf("%s ", toon[0].fname);
  printf("%s ", toon[1].lname);
  printf("is %d years old\n", toon[2].age);
  return 0;
}
```

Unions in structures

Unions can be declared inside a struct definition to allow values of different data types to be stored at the same memory address during the progress of the program. The example below first uses a union to store a char value which is used in a comparison. Then the union is used to store an int value which is subsequently displayed in hexadecimal format.

```c
#include <stdio.h>

typedef struct
{
  union
  {
    int num;
    char letter;
  };
} info;

int main()
{
  info stored;    /* create a struct of the info type */

printf("Want to convert an integer to hex? [Y or N]");
scanf("%c", &stored.letter );

  if( stored.letter == 'y' || stored.letter == 'Y')
  {
    printf("OK, enter the integer to be converted: ");
    scanf("%d", &stored.num );
    printf("%d in hex is 0x%X\n",stored.num,stored.num);
  }
  return 0;
}
```

useunion.c

Hot tip

The hexadecimal numbering system is informally referred to as "hex".

```
Command Prompt                             _ □ ✗
C:\MyPrograms>gcc useunion.c -o useunion.exe

C:\MyPrograms>useunion
Want to convert an integer to hex? [ Y or N ]: y
OK, enter the integer to be converted: 1024
1024 in hex is 0x400

C:\MyPrograms>_
```

Pointing to unions

A pointer to a union can be created in the same manner in which a pointer to a struct is created.

The example below defines a union type that can contain an int, char or float value. A union and a pointer are declared then various values are assigned to the union. Each one is assigned to the regular union then retrieved by the pointer, using the arrow operator.

unionptr.c

```c
#include <stdio.h>

typedef union
{
  int num;
  char *str;
  float dec;
} info;

int main()
{
  info uniondata; /* declare union of the info type */
  info *ptr;      /* & union pointer of the info type */
  ptr = &uniondata; /* now point to the first union */

  uniondata.num = 5;
  printf("The union value is now: %d\n", ptr->num );
  uniondata.str = "five";
  printf("The union value is now: %s\n", ptr->str );
  uniondata.dec = 0.125;
  printf("The union value is now: %f\n", ptr->dec );
  return 0;
}
```

Hot tip

Unions can be passed to functions in the same way that structures can be passed to functions – see the example on page 129.

```
C:\MyPrograms>gcc unionptr.c -o unionptr.exe

C:\MyPrograms>unionptr
The union value is now: 5
The union value is now: five
The union value is now: 0.125000

C:\MyPrograms>
```

134

Reading & writing files

This chapter introduces the "FILE" data type and demonstrates how it may be used to create and modify text files in a C program.

Creating a file

A special data type for handling files is defined in the stdio.h header file. It is called a file pointer and has the syntax FILE *. File pointers are used to open, read, write and close files.

In a C program a file pointer variable called "file_ptr" can be created with this declaration:

```
FILE *file_ptr ;
```

A file pointer points to a structure defined in the stdio.h header file that contains information about the file. This includes details about the current character and if the file is being read or written.

Before a file can be read or written it firstly must always be opened using the fopen() function. This takes two arguments which specify the name and location of the file, and a "mode" in which to open the file. The fopen() function returns a file pointer if successful, or NULL if the file cannot be opened.

The table below lists all the possible file modes that can be specified as the second argument to the fopen() function:

File mode	Operation
r	opens an existing file for reading
w	opens an existing file for writing – creates a new file if none exists or opens an existing file and discards all its previous contents
a	appends – opens or creates a text file for writing at the end of the file
r+	open a text file to read from or write to
w+	opens a text file to write to or read from
a+	opens or creates a text file to read from or write to at the end of the file

Where the mode includes a b after any of the file modes listed above, the operation relates to a binary file rather than a text file. For instance, rb or w+b.

Hot tip

All the standard functions for file input/output are contained in the stdio.h header file.

Don't forget

For convenience all the text files in the examples in this chapter are located in the MyPrograms folder that also contains the C source code files. On Windows the directory is C:\MyPrograms and on Linux systems it's at /home/MyPrograms.

This statement attempts to open a file called "data.txt", for writing only, and assign the returned file pointer to a file pointer variable:

```
FILE *file_ptr;

file_ptr = fopen("data.txt" , "w" );
```

The file pointer variable can be tested for a NULL value to determine if the attempt to open the file was successful – if the file pointer variable contains a NULL value the attempt has failed.

Once a file has been successfully opened it can be read, or added to, or new text can be written in the file, depending on the mode specified in the call to the fopen() function. Following this the open file must then always be closed with the fclose() function, which takes the file pointer variable as its single argument.

This example creates a new empty text file called "data.txt" in the MyPrograms directory:

```c
#include <stdio.h>
int main()
{
  FILE *file_ptr;          /* 1.declare a FILE pointer */
  file_ptr = fopen("data.txt", "w"); /*2.create file*/

  if( file_ptr != NULL)                    /* 3.test */
  {
    printf( "File created\n" );
    fclose(file_ptr); /*4.remember to close the file*/
    return 0;
  }
  else
  { printf( "Unable to create file.\n" ); return 1; }
}
```

Beware

Notice that both file name and file mode arguments must be enclosed by double quotes.

newfile.c

Command Prompt

```
C:\MyPrograms>gcc newfile.c -o newfile.exe

C:\MyPrograms>newfile
File created

C:\MyPrograms>_
```

Hot tip

Notice that this program returns a value of 1 to the system when the attempt to open the file fails – this tells the system that all did not go well.

Input & output file streams

Standard input

The scanf() function, used in previous examples, is the simplified version of a function named fscanf() which requires an input file stream as its first argument. This indicates a source from where a series of characters will be introduced into the program.

In C programming, the file stream named stdin represents the keyboard and is the default source for the scanf() function. The function call scanf(...) is the same as fscanf(stdin, ...).

Standard output

Similarly, the printf() function is the simplified version of a function named fprintf() which requires an ouput file stream as its first argument. This indicates a destination where a series of characters will be output from the program.

The file stream named stdout represents the monitor and is the default source for the printf() function. The function call printf(...) is the same as fprintf(stdout, ...).

Other standard functions, which have stdin or stdout as their default file streams, also have equivalents allowing an alternative file stream to be specified. These can be used to read files by specifying a file pointer as an alternative to reading from the stdin file stream. They can also be used to write files by specifying a file pointer as an alternative to the stdout file stream.

Hot tip

Another standard output file stream is named stderr, which is used to output error messages to the monitor.

- The fputc() function can be used to write to a file stream one character at a time, and its companion fgetc() can be used to read from a file stream one character at a time.

- The fputs() function can be used to write to a file stream one line at a time, and its companion fgets() can be used to read from a file stream one line at a time.

- The fread() function can be used to read an entire file stream, and its partner fwrite() can write an entire file stream.

- The fscanf() function and the fprintf() functions can be used to read and write file streams with strings and numbers.

Each one of these functions is used in the examples in this chapter to demonstrate reading and writing files.

Writing characters

The fputc() function can be used to write text into an open text file one character at a time. It is generally used in a loop which moves through each character element of a char array. The fputc() function takes two arguments to specify the character to write then the file pointer of the open file in which to write.

The loop in the example below ends when the \0 null character is found in the array element tested on that iteration.

```c
#include <stdio.h>
int main()
{
  FILE *file_ptr;          /* 1.declare a FILE pointer */
  char text[50]= { "Text, one character at a time." };
  int i;
  file_ptr = fopen("chars.txt", "w"); /* 2.open file*/

  if(file_ptr != NULL)                      /* 3.test */
  {
    printf( "File chars.txt created.\n" );
    for( i = 0 ; text[i] ; i++ )
    {
      fputc( text[i], file_ptr );  /* 4. write text */
    }
    fclose(file_ptr); /*5.remember to close the file*/
    return 0;
  }
  else
  { printf( "Unable to create file.\n" ); return 1; }
}
```

writechars.c

Hot tip

The fputc() function returns the ASCII code of the current character, or a constant called EOF denoting that the end of the file is reached.

139

Reading characters

The fgetc() function can be used to read text from an open text file one character at a time. It is generally used in a loop which moves through each character of the file stream until it encounters the EOF end of file constant. The fgetc() function takes a single argument of the file pointer of an open file from which to read.

The example below opens the text file created in the previous example and displays its contents to stdout using printf().

The loop in this example ends on the iteration where the EOF constant is found in the char variable named "next".

readchars.c

```c
#include <stdio.h>
int main()
{
  char next;
  FILE *file_ptr;          /* 1.declare a FILE pointer  */
  file_ptr = fopen("chars.txt", "r"); /* 2.open file*/

  if( file_ptr != NULL )                    /* 3.test */
  {
    printf( "File chars.txt opened.\nContents: " );
    while(1)
    {
      next = fgetc( file_ptr );      /* 4.read text */
      if( next != EOF )printf( "%c", next );
      else break;
    }
    fclose(file_ptr); /*5.remember to close the file*/
    return 0;
  }
  else
  { printf( "Unable to open file.\n" ); return 1; }
}
```

Hot tip

Note that the conditional test in the while loop is simply a 1 (one) – this loop would continue infinitely without the break statement.

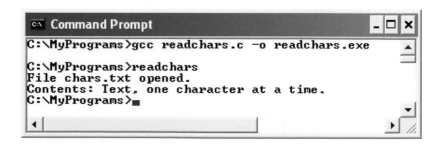

```
Command Prompt                                    _ □ ✕
C:\MyPrograms>gcc readchars.c -o readchars.exe

C:\MyPrograms>readchars
File chars.txt opened.
Contents: Text, one character at a time.
C:\MyPrograms>_
```

Reading lines

The fgetc() function is not the most efficient way of reading text into a program because it must be called repeatedly to read each character. It is better to use the fgets() function that reads text one line at a time.

The fgets() function takes three arguments. The first specifies a char pointer, or the name of a sized char array, to which the text will be assigned. The second is an int specifying the maximum number of characters to read per line. The third is a file pointer specifying where the program will read from.

```c
#include <stdio.h>
int main()
{
  char text[10];
  FILE *file_ptr;          /* 1.declare a FILE pointer */
  file_ptr = fopen("more.txt", "r");  /* 2.open file*/

  if( file_ptr != NULL )                    /* 3.test */
  {
   printf( "File more.txt opened.\nContents:\n" );
   while(fgets(text,10,file_ptr)!=NULL)/*4.read text*/
   {
     printf("%s", text);
   }
   fclose(file_ptr);  /*5.remember to close the file*/
   return 0;
  }
  else
  { printf( "Unable to open file.\n" ); return 1; }
}
```

readlines.c

141

Hot tip

This example opens a text file called "more.txt" that contains these three lines of text –
"Line one
Line two
Line three".
Each line is read into the char array named text and then written out on each iteration of the while loop.

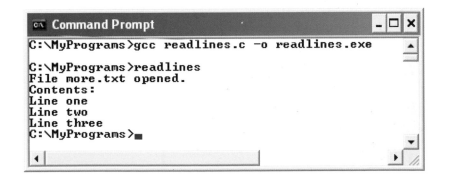

```
C:\MyPrograms>gcc readlines.c -o readlines.exe

C:\MyPrograms>readlines
File more.txt opened.
Contents:
Line one
Line two
Line three
C:\MyPrograms>
```

Writing lines

The fputc() function is not the most efficient method for writing large strings of text because the function is called repeatedly to write each individual character. A better method employs the fputs() function that writes the text line by line.

The fputs() function takes two arguments that specify a char pointer to a string, then a file pointer to the file in which to write. A newline character is added by fputs() after the string is written. This function returns zero when successful, or the EOF constant when an error occurs or the end of the file is reached. This example writes the line "Text," then the line "one line at a time.":

writelines.c

```c
#include <stdio.h>
int main()
{
   FILE *file_ptr;          /* 1.declare a FILE pointer */
   char *text = { "Text,\none line at a time." };
   int i;
   file_ptr = fopen("lines.txt", "w"); /* 2.open file*/

   if( file_ptr != NULL )                   /* 3.test */
   {
     printf( "File lines.txt created.\n" );
     fputs( text, file_ptr );         /* 4. write text */
     fclose(file_ptr); /*5.remember to close the file*/
     return 0;
   }
   else
   { printf( "Unable to create file.\n" ); return 1; }
}
```

Hot tip

The text string need not include a \n newline escape character.

Appending to a file

Specifying a file mode of "a" when opening a file means that any text then written to that file will be added after any existing text.

The program below reopens the text file used by the example on the opposite page. Next the user is asked to enter some text to be appended to the contents of that file. This is assigned to a char array by the gets() function, that uses the stdin file stream by default.

Finally the contents of the char array are appended to the existing contents of the open text file by the fputs() function.

```c
#include <stdio.h>
int main()
{
  char text[50];
  FILE *file_ptr;          /* 1.declare a FILE pointer */
  file_ptr = fopen("lines.txt", "a"); /* 2.open file*/

  if( file_ptr != NULL )                    /* 3.test */
  {
    printf( "File opened.\nEnter text to append: " );
    gets(text);
    fputs(text, file_ptr);           /* 4. write text */
    fclose(file_ptr); /*5.remember to close the file*/
    return 0;
  }
  else
  { printf( "Unable to open file.\n" ); return 1; }
}
```

append.c

Reading & writing entire files

Whole text files can be read and written with the fread() and fwrite() functions. Both of these functions take the same four arguments. The first is a char variable where the text can be stored. The second argument specifies the size of the chunks of text to read, or write, at a time – normally this will be 1. The third argument specifies the total number of characters to read or write, and the fourth argument is a file pointer to the file to work with.

This example creates a new text file named "dest.txt" and opens a file named "source.txt", whose contents are displayed below:

The fread() function assigns the entire text of source.txt to a char array named "buffer" and it assigns the sum total number of its characters to an int variable named "num".

The fwrite() function writes the entire contents of the buffer char array into the dest.txt file, shown on the opposite page.

When the copying operation has completed the total number of characters copied is displayed to stdout by the printf() function.

Hot tip

Use the number returned by fread() as the third argument to fwrite() to ensure that the number of characters read will be the same as those written.

readwrite.c
(part of)

```c
#include <stdio.h>

int main()
{
    FILE *src_ptr;              /* 1.declare file pointers */
    FILE *dest_ptr;

    char buffer[1000];
    int num;

    src_ptr  = fopen("source.txt","r"); /*2.open files*/
    dest_ptr = fopen( "dest.txt", "w");
```

```
if((src_ptr !=NULL) && (dest_ptr !=NULL)) /*3.test*/
{
  num =fread(buffer,1,1000,src_ptr); /*4.read text*/

  fwrite(buffer, 1, num, dest_ptr); /*5.write text*/

  fclose(src_ptr);/* 6.remember to close the files*/
  fclose(dest_ptr);

  printf("Finished: source.txt copied to dest.txt");
  printf("\n%d characters copied\n", num);
  return 0;
}
else
{
  if( src_ptr == NULL)
          printf("Unable to open source.txt\n");
  if( dest_ptr == NULL)
          printf("Unable to create dest.txt\n");
  return 1;
}
}
```

readwrite.c
(continued)

Beware

Ensure that the third argument to fread() is big enough to allow all the contents to be copied – changing the 1000 value to 100 would make this program only copy the first 100 characters of the text.

145

Don't forget

The char array storing the text must be large enough to accommodate all its characters.

Scanning input

The scanf() function, used to get user input, is the simplified version of the fscanf() function, with its file stream set to stdin. It has an advantage when reading files containing just numbers – numbers in a text file are simply seen as string characters, but when read by fscanf() they can be converted to their numeric type.

For instance, the program below reads the contents of a text file named "nums.txt". This contains the numbers 1-10, each separated by a space. Because fscanf() stops reading when it finds a space, the numbers can easily be assigned to an int array.

```c
#include <stdio.h>

int main()
{
  FILE *file_ptr;
  int nums[30], i, j;

  file_ptr = fopen("nums.txt", "r");
  if(file_ptr != NULL)
  {
    printf("File nums.txt opened.\n");
    for( i = 0; !feof(file_ptr); i++ )
          fscanf( file_ptr, "%d", &nums[i] );
    printf("Total numbers found: %d\n", i);
    printf("Numbers: ");
    for( j = 0 ; j < i ; j++) printf("%d ", nums[j]);
    fclose(file_ptr);
    return 0;
  }
  else
  { printf("Unable to open file.\n"); return 1; }
}
```

Don't forget

fscanf() takes the same arguments as scanf() plus a first argument that is a file pointer.

fscanf.c

Hot tip

The function named feof() is used to check for the end of a file – it takes a file pointer as its argument and returns 1 if the end of the file has been reached, or 0 if it hasn't. It is used here to end a loop when the end of the file is encountered.

```
C:\MyPrograms>gcc fscanf.c -o fscanf.exe

C:\MyPrograms>fscanf
File nums.txt opened.
Total numbers found: 10
Numbers: 1 2 3 4 5 6 7 8 9 10
C:\MyPrograms>
```

Printing output

The printf() function, used to write output, is the simplified version of the fprintf() function, with its file stream set to stdout.

The fprintf() function is used just like printf() but takes an additional first argument to specify a file stream to write to.

The example below writes a text string to new text file, pointed to by a file pointer variable, then writes the same string to the monitor, indicated by the stdout file stream.

```c
#include <stdio.h>

int main()
{
  FILE *file_ptr;
  char *hint= "fscanf() and fprintf() are more
        flexible \nthan other input/output functions.";

  file_ptr = fopen("hint.txt", "w");

  if(file_ptr != NULL)
  {
    printf( "File hint.txt created\n" );
    fprintf( file_ptr, "%s\n", hint );
    fprintf( stdout, "%s\n", hint );
    fclose(file_ptr);
    return 0;
  }
  else
  { printf( "Unable to open file.\n" ); return 1; }
}
```

fprintf.c

Hot tip

Unlike other input/output functions the fscanf() and fprintf() functions provide the ability to use format specifiers.

Reporting errors

The C language provides a function named perror() in the stdio.h header file that can be used to print descriptive error messages. It takes a string as its sole argument to which perror() adds a colon followed by a description of a current error.

Also the errno.h header file defines an integer expression named "errno" that is assigned an error code number when an error occurs. The errno value can be assigned as the argument to a function named strerror() to display its associated error message.

The program below demonstrates how perror() can be useful to explain an error that occurs when trying to open a missing file. It then continues with a loop displaying a few error code messages.

errno.c

```c
#include <stdio.h>

int main ()
{
  FILE * file_ptr;
  int i;

  file_ptr = fopen ("nonexistent.file", "r");
  if ( file_ptr == NULL ) perror ("Error");
      else fclose (file_ptr);

  printf( "\nSome error codes...\n" );
  for( i = 1; i < 6; i++ )
      printf("Error %d: %s\n", i, strerror(i) );

  return 0;
}
```

Hot tip

The range of error code messages associated with the errno integer vary from system to system – increase the loop maximum, to say 200, then run this program on your own system to see the full range. Trying this on Windows XP produced 42 messages whereas on Mandriva Linux it produced 124 error messages.

```
C:\MyPrograms>gcc errno.c -o errno.exe

C:\MyPrograms>errno
Error: No such file or directory

Some error codes...
Error 1: Operation not permitted
Error 2: No such file or directory
Error 3: No such process
Error 4: Interrupted function call
Error 5: Input/output error

C:\MyPrograms>
```

12 Interesting functions

This chapter introduces some interesting standard C functions and demonstrates random number generation, date & time manipulation, and memory management.

Getting the date & time

The current time on your system is generally counted as the number of seconds elapsed since 00:00:00 GMT on January 1, 1970 – a point in time known as the "Epoch". The total count represents the current date and time according to the Gregorian calendar and is referred to as "Calendar time". In C programming the time.h header file contains a range of special functions to handle time and date. This includes a function named time() that can be used to get the current Calendar time. This is returned as a special data type named time_t which is used to point to Calendar time values. The time() function requires a single argument which is normally the NULL constant, like this:

```
time_t calendar_time;
calendar_time = time(NULL);
```

Whilst Calendar time may be useful for calculations it is not the way that date and time are normally represented in everyday use. Calendar time can, however, be broken down into a binary representation of year, month, day, hour, and so on. This will also account for time zones to produce a useful local time. The time.h header file defines a data type struct named tm for the purpose of storing local time, with the components listed in the table below:

Component	Description
int tm_sec	seconds after the minute, normally 0 – 59
int tm_min	minutes after the hour, 0 – 59
int tm_hour	hours since midnight, 0 – 23
int tm_mday	day of the month, 1 – 31
int tm_mon	months since January, 0 – 11
int tm_year	years since 1900
int tm_wday	days since Sunday, 0 – 6
int tm_yday	days since January 1st, 0 – 365
int tm_isdst	is Daylight Saving Time in effect

A function named localtime() is used to break down a Calendar time into the components of the tm struct. This takes the Calendar time pointed to by a time_t data type as its single argument and returns a pointer to a local time.

The components of a local time can be formatted to strings in a number of ways. The simplest method uses a function named asctime() to convert the components into a standard format. This requires the local time tm struct as its argument.

The program below demonstrates each of these steps and displays both the Calendar time and formatted local time:

```c
#include <stdio.h>

#include <time.h>

int main()
{
  /*declare variables for calendar and local time */
  time_t  calendar_time;
  struct tm *local_time;

  /* get the current calendar time. */
  calendar_time = time(NULL);
  printf("%d seconds since the Epoch\n",calendar_time);

  /* convert calendar time to local time */
  local_time = localtime( &calendar_time );

  /* display date and time in the standard format. */
  printf("It's now: %s\n", asctime( local_time ) );
  return 0;
}
```

timenow.c

Beware

Notice that the & addressof operator is used in the conversion to local time in order to get the Calendar time from the time_t data type.

```
C:\MyPrograms>gcc timenow.c -o timenow.exe

C:\MyPrograms>timenow
1210061576 seconds since the Epoch
It's now: Tue May 06 09:12:56 2008

C:\MyPrograms>
```

Setting date & time formats

Selected local time components can be formatted with the strftime() function. This allows special time format specifiers to be applied and works much like the printf() and scanf() functions. The strftime() function takes four arguments to specify a char container where the string is to be assigned, the string size, the string itself and any format specifiers, and the local time to use.

This example first displays a time in the standard format then selects particular components to be displayed in a specified format:

timefmt.c

Hot tip

A full list of all the time format specifiers is included in the Reference section, on page 183.

```c
#include <stdio.h>
#include <time.h>
#define SIZE 256

int main()
{
  char buffer[SIZE];
  time_t  calendar_time;
  struct tm *local_time;
  calendar_time = time(NULL);
  local_time = localtime( &calendar_time );
  printf("It's now: %s\n", asctime( local_time ) );
  strftime (buffer,SIZE,"Day: %A\n",local_time);
  printf("%s",buffer);
  strftime(buffer,SIZE,"Date: %d %B %Y\n",local_time);
  printf("%s",buffer);
  strftime(buffer,SIZE,"Time: %H:%M %p\n",local_time);
  printf("%s",buffer);
  return 0;
}
```

```
Command Prompt                              _ □ ✕
C:\MyPrograms>gcc timefmt.c -o timefmt.exe

C:\MyPrograms>timefmt
It's now: Tue May 06 09:28:30 2008

Day: Tuesday
Date: 06 May 2008
Time: 09:09 AM

C:\MyPrograms>_
```

Using a timer

Getting the current time both before and after an event means that the duration of the event can be calculated by their difference. The time.h header file includes a function named difftime() for this particular purpose. The difftime() function takes two arguments of time_t data types. It subtracts the second argument from the first and returns the difference expressed in seconds, as a double type.

The double named "diff" in this example is assigned the time duration of running a loop that makes one billion iterations.

```c
#include <stdio.h>
#include <time.h>
#define BILLION 1000000000

int main()
{
  time_t start_time, end_time;
  int i;
  float diff;

  printf("Timer started");
  start_time = time(NULL);          /* call 1st time() */
  for( i = 0; i < BILLION; i++ )    /* run a loop */
    if( i % 100000000 == 0 ) printf(".");
  end_time = time(NULL);            /* call 2nd time() */
  printf("Timer stopped\n");

  /* calculate the time difference */
  diff = difftime( end_time, start_time );
  printf("It took around %d seconds
                to run the loop\n", (int)diff );
  return 0;
}
```

timer.c

153

```
C:\MyPrograms>gcc timer.c -o timer.exe

C:\MyPrograms>timer
Timer started..........Timer stopped
It took around 27 seconds to run the loop

C:\MyPrograms>
```

Generating random numbers

The rand() function generates a "random" positive integer from 0 to a large value (at least 32,767) every time it is called. To set a range for the random numbers use the modulus operator to specify the maximum number. For instance, to set a range 0 to 9:

```
int r = ( rand() % 9 ) ;
```

To specify a lower limit for the range add it to the result of the expression. For instance, to set a range from 1 to 10:

```
int r = ( rand() % 9) + 1
```

The numbers generated by rand() are not truly random as the function generates the same sequence of numbers each time the program is executed.

In order for rand() to generate a different sequence of numbers the seed that starts the sequence must be specified. This is achieved by specifying an integer argument to a function named srand(), like this:

```
srand( 12345 ) ;
```

Setting the random seed with srand() at the beginning of a program ensures that calls to the rand() function will no longer generate the default sequence of numbers. However, although it will now generate a different sequence, it is still one that will be repeated each time the program is executed.

To generate a random sequence the argument to the srand() function must be something other than a static integer value. It is commonplace to seed the rand() function using the current time as the argument to srand(), like this:

```
srand( time( NULL ) ) ;
```

Now the sequence of numbers generated by rand() will be different on each occasion that the program is executed.

The example program on the opposite page uses the current time to seed the random number generator. It creates an array of integers, in order, from 0 to 49. Random numbers generated by rand(), in a range of 1 to 49, are used to shuffle the element values. This means that the array contains all the numbers 1 to 49, in a random order, and without repeating any number.

Don't forget

Both rand() and srand() are part of the stdio.h header file – but a program must #include the time.h header file to make the time() function available to set the random seed.

...cont'd

```c
#include <stdio.h>
#include <time.h>

int main()
{
  int i, r, temp, nums[50];        /* array of numbers */
  srand(time(NULL));/* seed random number generator */

  for (i=0; i< 50; i++) nums[i] = i;    /* fill 0-49 */

  for ( i = 1; i < 50; i++ )
  {
    r= (rand() % 49)+1; /* randomize positions 1-49 */
    temp = nums[i]; nums[i] = nums[r]; nums[r] = temp;
  }

  for(i=0; i< 50; i++)    /* show all element values */
  {
    printf("Elem[%d]:%d  ",i, nums[i]);
    (i % 4 != 0) ? printf("\t") : printf("\n");
  }

  printf("\n\nYour 6 lucky LOTTO numbers are: ");
  for( i = 1; i < 7; i++ ) printf("%d  ",nums[i]);

  return 0;
}
```

lotto.c

Hot tip

The line using the conditional operator in this code is just there to format the output into columns.

155

```
C:\MyPrograms>gcc lotto.c -o lotto.exe

C:\MyPrograms>lotto
Elem[0]:0
Elem[1]:33      Elem[2]:8       Elem[3]:24      Elem[4]:48
Elem[5]:18      Elem[6]:10      Elem[7]:20      Elem[8]:2
Elem[9]:12      Elem[10]:27     Elem[11]:15     Elem[12]:11
Elem[13]:26     Elem[14]:47     Elem[15]:1      Elem[16]:40
Elem[17]:23     Elem[18]:38     Elem[19]:9      Elem[20]:32
Elem[21]:37     Elem[22]:25     Elem[23]:3      Elem[24]:19
Elem[25]:34     Elem[26]:17     Elem[27]:5      Elem[28]:45
Elem[29]:13     Elem[30]:49     Elem[31]:16     Elem[32]:22
Elem[33]:6      Elem[34]:14     Elem[35]:36     Elem[36]:21
Elem[37]:41     Elem[38]:7      Elem[39]:4      Elem[40]:42
Elem[41]:46     Elem[42]:35     Elem[43]:39     Elem[44]:31
Elem[45]:29     Elem[46]:44     Elem[47]:30     Elem[48]:43
Elem[49]:28

Your 6 lucky LOTTO numbers are: 33  8  24  48  18  10
C:\MyPrograms>
```

Don't forget

Element 0 is assigned the value zero and that element is never shuffled.

Allocating memory

Memory can be allocated dynamically with the malloc() function and released when it is no longer needed using the free() function.

The malloc() function requires an integer value as its argument to specify how many bytes of memory it should reserve, and it returns a pointer to the allocated space. The free() function takes the pointer to the space as its argument. It is good practice to always release memory when it is no longer needed.

The example below demonstrates how malloc() can be used to allocate memory space based on a user-specified size:

malloc.c

```c
#include <stdio.h>
#include <stdlib.h>

int main ()
{
  int num, i;
  char * buffer;

  printf ("This program generates a random string\n");
  printf ("How long do you want the string to be? ");
  scanf ( "%d", &num );
  /* allocate space 1 byte more than user input */
  buffer = ( char* ) malloc( num+1 );
  for( i = 0; i < num; i++ )
                            buffer[i]=(rand() % 26) + 'a';
  buffer[num] = '\0';
  printf ("Your random string is \'%s\'\n", buffer );
  free ( buffer );
  return 0;
  }
}
```

If the malloc() function cannot reserve the space requested the function returns a NULL value. This should be tested for when using malloc() to allow for that eventuality.

In the following example, the malloc() function reserves memory space for a user-specified quantity of integers. As the number of bytes used to store integers vary from system to system the sizeof() operator is used to calculate the total number of bytes to reserve.

```c
#include <stdio.h>
#include <stdlib.h>

int main()
{
  int qty, *numbers, i;

  printf("How many integers would you like to store?");
  scanf( "%d", &qty );
  numbers = malloc( qty * sizeof(int) );
  if( numbers != NULL )
  {
    for(i = 0; i < qty ; i++ ) numbers[i] = i+1;
    for(i = 0; i < qty ; i++) printf("%d ",numbers[i]);
    printf("\n");
    free(numbers);                /* free allocated memory */
    return 0;
  }
  else
  { printf( "!!! Insufficient memory\n" ); return 1; }
}
```

mallocint.c

Hot tip

This example does not need a cast because the pointer whose size is being set is an int data type.

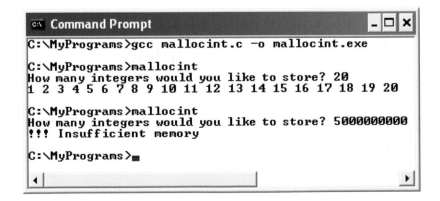

157

More memory management

There is another function in the stdlib.h header file that is very similar to the malloc() function described on the previous page. This one is named calloc() and has just two differences to the malloc() function.

Firstly, rather than the single argument required by malloc(), the calloc() function takes two integer arguments. These are multiplied together to specify how much memory space to allocate. Secondly, it clears all the allocated memory space to zero whereas malloc() leaves whatever values may already be there.

The differences can be clearly seen in this example:

calloc.c

```c
#include <stdio.h>
#include <stdlib.h>

int main()
{
  int *ptr1, *ptr2, i;
  ptr1 = calloc( 10, sizeof(int) );
  ptr2 = malloc( 10 );
  for( i = 0; i < 10; i++ )
  {
    printf("calloc no.%d: %d\t", i, ptr1[i] );
    printf("malloc no.%d: %d\n", i, ptr2[i] );
  }
  return 0;
}
```

Hot tip

The calloc() function returns NULL if the request to allocate memory fails – just like the malloc() function does. This should normally be tested to allow for that eventuality, as in the previous example.

```
Command Prompt                                    _ □ ×

C:\MyPrograms>gcc calloc.c -o calloc.exe

C:\MyPrograms>calloc
calloc no.0: 0    malloc no.0: 3998960
calloc no.1: 0    malloc no.1: 3998960
calloc no.2: 0    malloc no.2: 808335648
calloc no.3: 0    malloc no.3: 1262768928
calloc no.4: 0    malloc no.4: 196716
calloc no.5: 0    malloc no.5: 7078002
calloc no.6: 0    malloc no.6: 3998936
calloc no.7: 0    malloc no.7: 3998936
calloc no.8: 0    malloc no.8: 1330536272
calloc no.9: 0    malloc no.9: 1397704799

C:\MyPrograms>_
```

Memory that has been originally allocated a certain space with malloc() or calloc() can be increased with the realloc() function.

The example below uses the realloc() function to extend the memory allocated from its initial block of 5 to a larger block of 8:

```c
#include <stdio.h>
#include <stdlib.h>

int main()
{
  int i, *arr;

  arr = calloc( 5, sizeof(int) );
  if(arr != NULL )
  {
    printf("Enter 5 integers, separated by a space:");
    for( i = 0; i < 5; i++ ) scanf( "%d", &arr[i] );
    printf("Adding more space...\n");
    arr = realloc( 8, sizeof(int) );
    printf("Enter 3 more integers separated by a space:");
    for( i = 5; i < 8; i++ ) scanf( "%d", &arr[i] );
    printf("Thanks.\nYour 8 entries were: ");
    for( i = 0; i < 8; i++ ) printf( "%d, ", arr[i] );
    printf("\n");
    free(arr);
    return 0;
  }
  else
  { printf( "!!! Insufficient Memory\n" ); return 1; }
}
```

realloc.c

Hot tip

Like calloc(), the realloc() function takes two arguments to specify the size of the memory space – and it returns a pointer when successful or a NULL value if it fails.

```
Command Prompt                          _ □ ✕
C:\MyPrograms>gcc realloc.c -o realloc.exe

C:\MyPrograms>realloc
Enter 5 integers, separated by a space:1 2 3 4 5
Adding more space...
Enter 3 more integers separated by a space:6 7 8
Thanks.
Your 8 entries were: 1, 2, 3, 4, 5, 6, 7, 8,

C:\MyPrograms>_
```

What next?

This book will, hopefully, have given you a good understanding of the C programming language to the ANSI C standard. Like any language, be it a spoken language or a programming language, the best way to become proficient is to practice using it.

The Reference section in this book contains details of every function contained in the ANSI C library header files. It would be useful to experiment with each one so as to understand them better.

Creating C programs with a graphical user interface (GUI), such as applications for Windows, adds a lot of files to a program and these are best managed as a "Project" by a dedicated Integrated Development Environment (IDE).

Because the C++ language is an extension of the C language any IDE for C++ is also suitable for working with C programming. This does not necessarily mean that you have to know anything about the C++ programming language – you can simply use any C++ IDE to create C programs without regard to C++.

The Borland C++ Builder IDE (see **www.borland.com**) is favored by many C programmers, but it has extensions to the ANSI C standard that may result in less portable C program code.

Another great alternative is Microsoft's Visual C++ IDE. This has latterly been incorporated into the Microsoft Visual Studio package, which requires an NT, Windows 2000, XP, or Vista platform – so Windows 95, 98 and ME users cannot enjoy its benefits.

The full-blown version of Visual Studio includes many different development tools, for C++, Visual Basic, and the latest language of C# (pronounced "see-sharp"). Earlier versions of the Microsoft Visual C++ 6 IDE can still be found for Windows 9.x. This is a great C/C++ development tool – at a lower cost too!

There is also a GUI front-end, for the GNU compiler used in this book, available free from BloodshedSoftware – for download at **www.bloodshed.net**. This free IDE is highly acclaimed – it's available for both Windows and Linux users, and you can't argue about the price.

You may, however, choose none of these options, and still enjoy a great future with C – it's around to stay. Happy C programming!

Reference section

This section of the book lists the standard ASCII key codes and every function contained in the standard C library, grouped by their header file, and also descriptions of all the standard constants.

ASCII character codes

ASCII (American Standard Code for Information Interchange) is the standard representation of characters by numerical code. The non-printing character codes, originally developed for teletypes, are now rarely used for their intended original purpose.

There are also extended ASCII code sets from 128-255 (not listed) containing accented characters and symbols, but these sets do vary.

Note that the character represented by the character code 32 is not missing – it is, in fact, the non-printing space character. Also the character represented by character code 127 is the delete character.

Code	Char	Description	Code	Char	Description
0	NUL	null	16	DLE	data link escape
1	SOH	start of heading	17	DC1	device control 1
2	STX	start of text	18	DC2	device control 2
3	ETX	end of text	19	DC3	device control 3
4	EOT	end of transmission	20	DC4	device control 4
5	ENQ	enquiry	21	NAK	neg. acknowledge
6	ACK	acknowledgement	22	SYN	synchronous file
7	BEL	bell	23	ETB	end of trans. block
8	BS	backspace	24	CAN	cancel
9	TAB	horizontal tab	25	EM	end of medium
10	NL	newline	26	SUB	substitute
11	VT	vertical tab	27	ESC	escape
12	FF	form feed	28	FS	file separator
13	CR	carriage return	29	GS	group separator
14	SO	shift out	30	RS	record separator
15	SI	shift in	31	US	unit separator

Code	Char	Code	Char	Code	Char	Code	Char
32		56	8	80	P	104	h
33	!	57	9	81	Q	105	i
34	"	58	:	82	R	106	j
35	#	59	;	83	S	107	k
36	$	60	<	84	T	108	l
37	%	61	=	85	U	109	m
38	&	62	>	86	V	110	n
39	'	63	?	87	W	111	o
40	(	64	@	88	X	112	p
41	)	65	A	89	Y	113	q
42	*	66	B	90	Z	114	r
43	+	67	C	91	[	115	s
44	,	68	D	92	\	116	t
45	-	69	E	93	]	117	u
46	.	70	F	94	^	118	v
47	/	71	G	95	_	119	w
48	0	72	H	96	`	120	x
49	1	73	I	97	a	121	y
50	2	74	J	98	b	122	z
51	3	75	K	99	c	123	{
52	4	76	L	100	d	124		
53	5	77	M	101	e	125	}
54	6	78	N	102	f	126	~
55	7	79	O	103	g	127	del

Hot tip

To find out more about extended ASCII sets try the website at www.asciitable.com or search for ASCII on the web.

Hot tip

The term "ASCII" file just means a plain text file, such as those produced by Window's Notepad application.

Input & output functions

The functions and types defined in the stdio.h header represent almost one third of the C language library. It is used to introduce data into a program and generate output from a program.

A "stream" is a data source terminated by a "\n" newline character. It may be read or written by "opening" the stream, and terminated by "closing" it. Opening a stream returns a FILE type pointer in which information needed to control the stream is stored.

The functions listed in the following table perform file operations:

File-handling functions

FILE *fopen(const char *filename, const char mode)

The fopen() function returns a FILE pointer, or NULL if the file cannot be opened. Any of the following modes may be specified in the function call:

r   open a text file for reading only
w   create a text file to write to – and discard any previous contents
a   append – open or create a text file for writing at the end of the file
r+   open a text file to update (read and write)
w+   open a text file to update (read and write discarding any previous contents)
a+   append – open or create a text file for update, for writing at the end of the file

If the file being opened is a binary file a b should be added after the file mode, for instance wb+

FILE freopen(const char *filename const char mode
  FILE *stream)

The freopen() function opens a file with the specified mode and associates the stream with it. It returns the stream or NULL if an error occurs. This function is normally used to change the files associated with stdin, stdout or stderr

int fflush(FILE * stream)

On an output stream this function causes any buffered data to be written immediately. It returns the EOF constant for a write error, or zero otherwise. A call to fflush(NULL) flushes all output streams int fclose(FILE *stream)

A call to fclose() flushes any unwritten data from the stream then closes the stream. It returns the EOF constant if an error occurs, or zero otherwise

int remove(const char *filename)

This function removes the specified file – so that any subsequent attempt to open that file will fail. It returns a non-zero value if it cannot remove the file

int rename(const char *old-name, const char *new-name)

The rename() function changes the name of the specified file, or it returns a non-zero value if it cannot rename the file

FILE *tmpfile(void)

Calling tmpfile() creates a temporary file, with the file mode of wb+, that is removed when the program ends. This function returns a stream, or NULL if the file cannot be created

char *tmpnam(char arr [L_tmpnam])

This function stores a string in an array and returns a unique valid file name pointer to that array. The arr array must have at least L_tmpnam characters. The tmpnam() function generates a different name each time it is called

int setvbuf(FILE *stream, char *buffer, int mode, size_t size)

A call to setvbuf() sets buffering for the specified stream. It should be called after a stream has been opened but before any operation has been performed on it. Valid modes are _IOFBF to cause full buffering, _IOLBF for line buffering and _IONBF for no buffering. The size sets the buffer size. This function returns a non-zero value if an error occurs

void setbuf(FILE *stream, char *buffer)

The setbuf() function defines how a stream should be buffered. It should be called after a stream has been opened but before any operation has been performed on it. The argument buffer points to an array to be used as the buffer

**Functions that
format output**

int fprintf(FILE *stream, const char *format, ...)

The fprintf() function converts and writes output to a
specified file stream under the control of a format specifier.
It returns the number of characters written, or a negative
value if an error occurs

int printf(const char *format, ...)

The printf() function writes and converts output to stdout.
It is equivalent to fprintf(stdout, const char *format, ...)

int sprintf(char *s, const char *format, ...)

The sprintf() function is the same as printf() except the
output is written into the specified string, and terminated
with a \0 null character

vprintf(const char *format, va_list arg)
vfprintf(FILE *stream, const char *format, va_list arg)
vsprintf(char *s, const char *format, va_list arg)

These three functions are equivalent to the corresponding
printf() functions except that their variable argument list is
replaced by an argument of the va_list type. Refer to the
stdarg.h header file functions on page 180 for more details

**Functions that
format input**

int fscanf(FILE *stream, const char *format, ...)

The fscanf() function reads from a specified stream under
the control of a format specifier and assigns converted
values to subsequent arguments. It returns the number of
input items converted or the EOF constant if the end of the
file is met, or if an error occurs

int scanf(constant char *format, ...)

The scanf() function reads and converts input to stdin. It is
equivalent to fscanf(stdin, const char *format, ...)

int sscanf(char *s, const char *format, ...)

The sscanf() function is the same as scanf() except the input
is read from the specified string

In C a "%" prefix denotes a format specifier. All printf() format specifiers are listed below, and those for scanf() on the next page.

Format specifiers for output

Character	printf() converts to
d,i	int data type, signed decimal
o	int data type, unsigned octal without a leading zero
x, X	int unsigned hexadecimal. 0x uses lowercase, such as 0xff, and 0X uses uppercase, such as 0XFF
u	int data type, unsigned decimal
c	int single character, after conversion to char data type
s	char pointer to a string, ending with the \0 null character
f	double data type in the form xxx.yyyyyy where the number of digits after the decimal point is set by precision. The default precision is 6 digits
e, E	double data type in the form xx.yyyyyye±zz or xx.yyyyyyE±zz where the number of digits after the decimal point is set by precision. The default precision is 6 digits
g, G	double data type printed as %e or %E conversion if the exponent is less than -, otherwise printed as a %f conversion
p	the memory address of a pointer
n	not a conversion, but stores the number of characters written so far by the call to the printf() function in an int pointer argument
%	not a conversion, prints a '%'

Format specifiers for input

Character	scanf() converts to
d	int data type, signed decimal integer
i	int data type which may be in octal (leading 0) or hexadecimal (leading 0x or 0X)
o	int data type, octal integer with or without a leading zero
u	int data type, unsigned decimal
x	int hexadecimal integer, with or without leading 0x or 0X
c	char characters, into a specified array. Reads the number of characters stated in its width field (default is 1) without adding a final \0 null character. Stops reading when a space is met
s	a string of non-whitespace char characters, into an array. The array must be big enough for all the characters plus a final \0 null character
e, f, g	float data type, optionally beginning with a sign, then followed by a string of numbers. These may contain a decimal point, and an optional exponent field containing an ""E"" or ""e"" followed by a possibly signed integer
p	a memory address, in the same form as that output by the %p conversion with printf()
n	not a conversion, but stores the number of characters read so far by the call to the scanf() function in an int pointer argument
[...]	matches a string specified in the square brackets to those in the input stream and adds a \0 null character
[^ ...]	matches all ASCII characters in the input stream except those specified in the square brackets, and adds a \0 null character

Functions for character input and output

int fgetc(FILE *stream)
returns the next character of the specified stream as a char, or the EOF constant if at the end of the file or an error occurs

char *fgets(char *s, int n, FILE *stream)

reads the next n-1 characters into the specified stream then adds a \0 null character at the end of the array. This function returns s or NULL if at the end of the file or if an error occurs

int fputc(int c, FILE *stream)
writes the character c to the specified stream and returns the character written or EOF if an error occurs

int fputs(const char *s, FILE *stream)

writes the string s to the specified stream and returns non-negative, of EOF if an error occurs

int getc(FILE *stream)
the getc() function is the macro equivalent of fgetc()

int getchar(void)
the getchar() function is equivalent to getc(stdin)

char *gets(char *s)

reads the next input line into an array, replacing its final newline character with a \0 null character. It returns s or NULL if at the end of the file, or if an error occurs

int putc(int c, FILE *stream)
the putc() function is the macro equivalent of fputc()

int putchar(int c) is equivalent to putc(c, stdout)

int puts(const char *s)

writes the string s and a newline character to stdout. It returns non-negative or EOF if an error occurs

int ungetc(int c, FILE *stream)

pushes the character c back onto the specified stream where it is returned on the next read. Only one pushback character per stream is guaranteed and EOF cannot be pushed back. ungetc() returns the character pushed back, or EOF on error

**Functions for
direct stream
input and output**

The fread() and fwrite() functions contained in the stdio.h header file are most effective to read and write entire text files:

size_t fread(void *ptr, size_t size,
                          size_t nobj, FILE *stream)

the fread() function reads from the specified stream into the specified ptr array pointer at most nobj objects of size size. fread() returns the number of objects it has read, which may be less than the number requested in the function call

The status of fread() can be tested as it proceeds using the feof() and ferror() functions – see the error functions listed on the opposite page

size_t fwrite(const void *ptr, size_t size,
                          size_t nobj, FILE *stream)

the fwrite() function writes from the specified ptr pointer nobj objects of size size. It returns the number of objects that it has written. If an error occurs the returned value will be less than that requested by nobj in the function call

Many of the standard functions in the C library set status indicators when an error occurs, or when the end of a file is reached. These indicators can be tested using the error functions listed in the table below. Also the integer expression errno, defined in the errno.h header file, may contain an error code giving more information about the most recent error.

Error functions

void clearerr(FILE *stream)

the clearerr() function clears the end of file and error indicators for the specified stream

int feof(FILE *stream)

the feof() function returns a non-zero vale if the end of file indicator is set for the specified stream

int ferror(FILE *stream)

the ferror() function returns a non-zero value if the error indicator is set for the specified stream

void perror(const char *s)

the perror() function prints an implementation defined error message associated with the integer value contained in the errno expression. See also the strerror() function in the string.h header file on page 175

File-positioning functions

A file stream is processed by moving through the characters it contains one by one. The functions in the following table can be used to manipulate the position in a file stream:

int fseek(FILE *stream, long offset, int original)

the fseek() function sets the file position in the specified stream. Subsequent reading, or writing, begins at the new position. The new position is determined by specifying how far to offset the position from its original position. Optionally the third argument of the fseek() function can be specified as SEEK_SET (beginning), SEEK_CUR (current position) or SEEK_END (end of file). For a text stream the offset must be either zero or a value returned by the ftell() function with the original position specified as SEEK_SET. The fseek() function returns non-zero if an error occurs

long ftell(FILE *stream)

the ftell() function returns the current file position of the specified stream, or -1L if an error occurs

int fgetpos(FILE *stream, fpos_t *ptr)

the fgetpos() records the current file position of the specified stream in the specified ptr pointer as a special fpos_t type. This function returns a non-zero value if an error occurs

int fsetpos(FILE *stream, const fpos_t *ptr)

the fsetpos() function positions the file pointer in the specified stream at the position recorded by fgetpos() in the ptr pointer. fsetpos() returns a non-zero value on error

Character test functions

<ctype.h>

The ctype.h header file contains functions for testing characters. In each case, the character must be specified as the function's argument. The functions return a non-zero value (true) when the tested condition is met, or zero if it is not. Additionally, this header file contains two functions for converting the case of letters. All of the functions in the ctype.h header file are listed in the table below together with a description:

Function	Description
isalpha(c)	is the character a letter?
isalnum(c)	is the character a letter or a number?
iscntrl(c)	is the character a control character?
isdigit(c)	is the character a decimal digit?
isgraph(c)	is the character any printing character except a space?
islower(c)	is the character a lowercase letter?
isprint(c)	is the character any printing character including a space?
ispunct(c)	is the character any printing character except a space, a letter, or a digit?
isspace(c)	is the character a space, formfeed, newline, carriage return, horizontal tab, or vertical tab?
isupper(c)	is the character an uppercase letter?
isxdigit(c)	is the character a hexadecimal digit?
int tolower(int c)	convert the character to lowercase
int toupper(int c)	convert the character to uppercase

String functions

The string.h header file contains the following functions that can be used to compare and manipulate text strings:

Function	Description
char *strcpy(s1, s2)	copy s2 to s1, then return s1
char *strncpy(s1, s2, n)	copy n characters of s2 to s1, then return s1
char *strcat(s1, s2)	concatenate s2 to the end of s1, then return s1
char *strncat(s1, s2, n)	concatenate n characters of s2 to the end of s1, then return s1
int strcmp(s1, s2)	compare s1 to s2, then return < 0 if s1 < s2, 0 if s1== s2, or > 0 if s1 > s2
int strncmp(s1, s2, n)	compare n characters of s1 to s2, then return < 0 if s1 < s2, 0 if s1 == s2, or > 0 if s1 > s2
char *strchr(s, c)	return a pointer to the first occurrence of c in s, or NULL if not present
char *strrchr(s, c)	return a pointer to the last occurrence of c in s, or NULL if not present
size_t strspn(s1, s2)	return length of prefix of s1 consisting of characters in s2
size_t strcspn(s1, s2)	return length of prefix of s1 consisting of characters not in s2

Function	Description
char *strpbrk(s1, s2)	return a pointer to the first occurrence in s1 of any character of s2, or NULL if none are present
char *strstr(s1, s2)	return a pointer to the first occurrence of s2 in s1 or NULL if not present
size_t strlen(s)	return the length of s
char *strerror(n)	return a pointer to the implementation-defined string associated with error code n
char *strtok(s1, s2)	search s1 for tokens delimited by characters from s2
void *memcpy(s1, s2, n)	copy n characters from s2 to s1, then return s1
void *memmove(s1, s2, n)	same as memcpy() but it works even when the objects overlap
int memcmp(s1, s2, n)	compare the first n characters of s1 with s2, return as with the strcmp() function
void *memchr(s, c, n)	return a pointer to the first occurrence of character c in s, or return NULL if not present in the first n characters
void *memset(s, c, n)	place character c into the first n characters of s, then return s

Math functions

The math.h header file contains functions that perform mathematical calculations. All the functions are listed in the table below together with a description of the calculation they perform. In the table, x and y are double data types and *n* is a int data type. All the functions return the result of their calculation as a double data type:

Function	Description
sin(x)	return the sine of x
cos(x)	return the cosine of x
tan(x)	return the tangent of x
asin(x)	return the arcsine of x
acos(x)	return the arccosine of x
atan(x)	return the arctangent of x
atan2(y, x)	return the angle (in radians) from the x axis to a point y
sinh(x)	return the hyperbolic sine of x
cosh(x)	return the hyperbolic cosine of x
tanh(x)	return the hyperbolic tangent of x
exp(x)	return e (the base of natural logarithms) raised to the power x
log(x)	return the natural logarithm of x
log10(x)	return the base10 logarithm of x
pow(x, y)	return x raised to the power y
sqrt(x)	return the square root of x

Function	Description
ceil(x)	return the smallest integer not less than x, as a double
floor(x)	return the largest integer not greater than x, as a double
fabs(x)	return the absolute value of x
ldexp(x, n)	return x multiplied by 2 and raised to the power n
frexp(x, int *exp)	decompose x into two parts – return a mantissa between 0.5 and 1, and store exponent in exp
modf(x, double *ip)	split x into integer and fraction – return the fractional part, and store the integral part in ip
fmod(x, y)	return the remainder of dividing x by y

Utility functions

double atof(const char *s) converts s to a double

int atoi(const char *s) converts s to an int

long atol(const char *s) converts s to a long

double strtod(const char *s, char **endp)
converts the initial part of s to a double, ignoring leading
whitespace. A pointer to the rest of s is stored in *endp

long strtol(const char *s, char **endp, int b)
converts the initial part of s to a long using base b.
A pointer to the rest of s is stored in *endp

unsigned long strtoul(const char *s, char **endp, int b)
the strtoul() function is the same as the strtol() function
except that the returned result is an unsigned long

int rand(void)
returns a psuedo-random number between zero and an
implementation-dependent maximum of at least 32,767

void srand(unsigned int seed)
sets the seed for a new sequence of random numbers
supplied by rand(). The initial seed is 1

void *calloc(size_t nobj, size_t size)
returns a pointer to memory space for an array of nobj
objects of size size, or NULL if the request cannot be met.
This space is initialized to zero bytes

void *malloc(size_t size)
returns a pointer to memory space for an object of size
size, or NULL if the request fails. This space is uninitialized

void *realloc(void *p, size_t size)
changes the size of an object pointed to by p to size. realloc()
returns a pointer to the new space or NULL if the request fails

void free(void *p)
the free() function deallocates the memory space pointed
to by p. Note that p must be a pointer to memory space
previously allocated by calloc(), malloc() or realloc()

void abort(void) causes the program to end abnormally

void exit(int *status*)
causes the program to end normally. The value of *status*
is returned to the system. Optionally EXIT_SUCCESS and
EXIT_FAILURE can be used to specify the *status* values

int atexit(void (*fcn*) (void))
registers the function *fcn* to be called when the program
terminates. atexit() returns a non-zero value if unsuccessful

int system(const char *s*)
passes the string *s* to the environment for processing.
The return value is implementation-dependent

char *getenv(const char *name*)
returns the environment string associated with *name*,
or NULL if no string is associated with *name* in that
environment. The details are implementation-dependent

void *bsearch(const void *key*, const void *base*, size_t *n*,
size_t *size*, int (*cmp)(const void *keyval*, const void *datum*))

searches base[0]...base[*n*-1] for an item that matches *key*.
It returns a pointer to the matching item if successful,
otherwise it returns a NULL value. Items in the array base
must be in ascending order

void qsort(void *base*, size_t *n*, size_t *size*,
                 int(*cmp)(const void *, const void *))

sorts into ascending order an arraybase[0]...base[n-1] of
objects of size *size*. The comparison function cmp() is the
same as that in the bsearch() function

int abs(int *n*) returns the absolute value of int *n*

long labs(long *n*) returns the absolute value of long *n*

div_t ldiv(long *num*, long *denom*)
divides *num* by *denom* and stores the results in
members of a structure of type ldiv_t. Its quot member
stores the quotient result and its rem member stores the
remainder result

Diagnostic functions

The assert() function, contained in the assert.h header file, can be used to add diagnostics to a program:

```
void assert(int expression ) ;
```

If *expression* is zero when assert(*expression*) is executed, the function will print a message on stderr, such as:

```
Assertion failed: expression, file filename, line nnn
```

The assert() function then attempts to terminate the program.

<stdarg.h>

Argument functions

The stdarg.h header file contains functions that can be used to step through a list of function arguments without first knowing their number and type. Due to the nature of these functions, they must be implemented as "macros", within the function's body.

The list of arguments is assigned to a special data type named va_list. The functions listed in the following table manipulate a variable named "args" of the va_list type:

va_start(va_list *args*, lastarg)

must be called once to initialize the va_list named *args* at the position in the list of the last known argument *lastarg*

va_arg(va_list *args*, *data-type*)

after the va_list *args* has been initialized with va_start() each successive call to va_arg() will return the value of the next argument in the *args* list as the specified *data-type*

va_end(va_list *args*)

must be called once after the arguments in the va_list *args* have been processed, before the function is exited

Date & time functions

<time.h>

The time.h header file contains functions for manipulating date and time. Some of these functions process "Calendar time", which is based on the Gregorian calendar. This is stated in seconds elapsed since the Epoch (00:00:00 GMT January 1st, 1970).

Other functions contained in time.h process "Local time", which is the translation of Calendar time accounting for time zone.

The data type time_t is used to describe both Calendar time and Local time.

A struct named tm contains the components of Calendar time, which are listed in the following table:

Component	Description
int tm_sec	seconds after the minute, 0-61
int tm_min	minutes after the hour, 0-59
int_tm_hour	hours since midnight, 0-23
int tm_mday	day of the month, 1-31
int tm_mon	months since January, 0-11
int tm_year	years since 1900
int tm_wday	days since Sunday, 0-6
int tm_yday	days since January 1st, 0-365
int tm_isdst	Daylight Saving Time flag

The tm_isdst component is positive if Daylight Saving is in effect, zero if it is not, and negative if the information is unavailable.

The functions contained in the time.h header file are listed in the table on the next page.

The time.h header file contains the functions listed below that can be used to manipulate date and time:

clock_t clock(void)
returns the processor time used by the program since it started, or -1 if unavailable

time_t time(time_t *tp)
returns the current calendar time, or -1 if unavailable

double difftime(time_t time2, time_t time1)
returns time2-time1, expressed in seconds

time_t mktime(struct tm *tp)
converts the local time in the structure *tp into calendar time

char *asctime(const struct tm *tp)
converts the time in the struct *tp into a standard string

char *ctime(const time_t *tp)
converts calendar time to local time

struct tm *gmtime(const time_t *tp)
converts calendar time into Coordinated Universal Time (UTC or GMT)

struct tm *localtime(const time_t *tp)
converts the calendar time *tp into local time

size_t strftime(char *s, size_t smax, const char *fmt, const struct tm *tp)

formats the time *tp into a chosen format *fmt

The strftime() function formats selected components of the tm struct according to the stated format specifier. All the possible format specifiers that can be used with strftime() are listed in the table on the opposite page.

Specifier	Description
%a	abbreviated weekday name
%A	full weekday name
%b	abbreviated month name
%B	full month name
%c	local date and time representation
%d	day of the month, 01 - 31
%H	hour (24-hour clock), 00 - 23
%I	hour (12-hour clock), 01-12
%j	day of the year, 001 - 366
%m	month of the year, 01 - 12
%M	minute, 00 - 59
%p	local equivalent of AM or PM
%S	second, 00 - 61 (to account for leap seconds)
%U	week number of the year (Sunday as the first day of the week), 00 - 53
%w	weekday number, 0 - 6 (Sunday is 0)
%W	week number of the year (Monday as the first day of the week), 00 - 53
%x	local date representation
%X	local time representation
%y	year without century, 00 - 99
%Y	year with century
%Z	time zone name, if available

Jump functions

The setjmp.h header is used for controlling low-level calls and provides a means to avoid the normal call and return sequence.

int setjmp(jmp_buf *env*)

low-level function used in conditional tests to save the environment in the *env* variable, then return zero

void longjmp(jmp_buf *env*, int *value*)

restores an evironment that has been saved in the *env* variable by setjmp() – as if setjmp() had returned the *value*

<signal.h>

Signal functions

The signal.h header contains functions for handling exceptional conditions that may arise during the execution of a program:

void (*signal (int *sig*, void (**handler*) (int))) (int)
the signal() function specifies how subsequent signals will be handled. The handler can be SIG_DFL, an implementation-defined default, or SIG_IGN to ignore the signal.
Valid *sig* signals include:

    SIGABRT : abnormal termination
    SIGFPE : arithmetic error
    SIGILL : illegal instruction
    SIGINT : external interruption
    SIGSEGV : access outside memory limit
    SIGTERM : termination request sent to the program

The function returns the previous value of handler for that specific signal, or SIG_ERR if an error occurs. When a *sig* signal next occurs the signal is restored to its default behavior then the signal-handler is called. If this returns, execution resumes at the point where the signal occurred

int raise(int *sig*)
attempts to send the signal *sig* to the program and returns a non-zero value if the attempt is unsuccessful

Limit constants

<limits.h>

The table below lists constants related to maximum and minimum numerical limits. Their values vary according to implementation. Where a value is given, in brackets, it indicates a minimum size for that constant – but larger values may, in fact, be imposed. Programs should not assume that any implementation-dependent constant will be of a particular value.

Constant	Value
CHAR_BIT	number of bits in a char (8)
CHAR_MAX	maximum value of char (UCHAR_MAX or SCHAR_MAX)
CHAR_MIN	minimum value of char (zero or SCHAR_MIN)
INT_MAX	maximum value of int (+32,787)
INT_MIN	minimum value of int (-32,767)
LONG_MAX	maximum value of long (+2,147,483,647)
LONG_MIN	minimum value of long (-2,147,483,647)
SCHAR_MAX	maximum value of signedchar (+127)
SCHAR_MIN	minimum value of signedchar (-127)
SHRT_MAX	maximum value of short (+32,767)
SHRT_MIN	minimum value of short (-32,767)
UCHAR_MAX	maximum value of unsignedchar (+255)
UINT_MAX	maximum value of unsignedint (+65,535)
ULONG_MAX	maximum value of unsigned long (+4,294,967,295)
USHRT_MAX	maximum value of unsigned short (+65,535)

Float constants

The table below lists constants related to floating-point arithmetic. Their values vary according to implementation. Where a value is given, in brackets, it indicates a minimum size for that constant.

Constant	Value
FLT_RADIX	radix of float exponent representations (2)
FLT_ROUNDS	rounding to the nearest number
FLT_DIG	number of precision digits (6)
FLT_EPSILON	smallest number x, where $1.0 + x\ != 1.0$ (1E-5)
FLT_MANT_DIG	number of FLT_RADIX mantissa digits
FLT_MAX	maximum floating point number (1E+37)
FLT_MAX_EXP	largest number n, where $\text{FLT\_RADIX}^n - 1$ is a valid number
FLT_MIN	minimum floating point number (1E-37)
FLT_MIN_EXP	smallest number n where 10^n is valid
DBL_DIG	number of double precision digits (10)
DBL_EPSILON	smallest number x, where $1.0 + x\ != 1.0$ (1E-9)
DBL_MANT_DIG	number of FLT_RADIX mantissa digits
DBL_MAX	maximum double float number (1E+37)
DBL_MAX_EXP	largest number n, where $\text{FLT\_RADIX}^n - 1$ is a valid number
DBL_MIN	minimum double float number (1E-37)
DBL_MIN_EXP	smallest number n where 10^n is valid

Index

U

V

W